Lead Like the

Based on the popular presentation of the same name, *Lead Like the Legends* uses the inspiring words of musical legends to help teachers and administrators learn the principles of effective leadership.

The book is organized around 14 musical greats, including Ray Charles, Duke Ellington, Marian Anderson, Carlos Santana, the Beatles, Bob Dylan, and Louis Armstrong. As you examine the words of wisdom from these artists, you'll learn the keys to strong leadership, such as . . .

- being sincere;
- accepting no limits;
- leading with imagination;
- leading by participating;
- being daring and high energy;
- using teamwork; and
- being yourself.

Each chapter includes motivational stories and examples from school leaders across the country, as well as reflection activities, self-assessments, and planning tools to help you implement the ideas. Whether you're a teacher looking to enhance your skills or an administrator in charge of managing a school or district, you'll come away from the book with fresh ideas and inspiration to help you on your journey.

David I. Steinberg is Director of the Department of Professional Growth at Montgomery County Public Schools. He has previously served as principal at a number of elementary, middle, and high schools, and has taught at the elementary, middle, high school, and college levels. He presents on *Lead Like the Legends* to K–12 schools, as well as to district offices, all over the country.

Other Eye On Education
Books Available from Routledge

(www.routledge.com/eyeoneducation)

From School Administrator to School Leader
15 Keys to Maximizing Your Leadership Potential
Brad Johnson and Julie Sessions

What Great Principals Do Differently, 2nd Edition
18 Things That Matter Most
Todd Whitaker

What Great Teachers Do Differently, 2nd Edition
17 Things That Matter Most
Todd Whitaker

Dealing with Difficult Teachers, 3rd Edition
Todd Whitaker

Dealing with Difficult Parents, 2nd Edition
Todd Whitaker and Douglas J. Fiore

101 Answers for New Teachers and Their Mentors, 3rd Edition
Effective Teaching Tips for Daily Classroom Use
Annette Breaux

Making Good Teaching Great
Everyday Strategies for Teaching with Impact
Annette Breaux and Todd Whitaker

Motivating & Inspiring Teachers, 2nd Edition
The Educational Leader's Guide for Building Staff Morale
Todd Whitaker, Beth Whitaker, and Dale Lumpa

Teaching Matters, 2nd Edition
How to Keep Your Passion and Thrive in Today's Classroom
Todd Whitaker and Beth Whitaker

101 Poems for Teachers
Annette Breaux

To Andrea,

You are a leader who does inspiring work bringing people together on behalf of children and families.

David

March 7, 2016

Lead Like the Legends

Advice and Inspiration for Teachers and Administrators

David I. Steinberg

Routledge
Taylor & Francis Group

NEW YORK AND LONDON

First published 2016
by Routledge
711 Third Avenue, New York, NY 10017

and by Routledge
2 Park Square, Milton Park, Abingdon, Oxon OX14 4RN

Routledge is an imprint of the Taylor & Francis Group, an informa business

© 2016 Taylor & Francis

The right of David I. Steinberg to be identified as author
of this work has been asserted by him in accordance with
sections 77 and 78 of the Copyright, Designs and Patents
Act 1988.

All rights reserved. No part of this book may be reprinted
or reproduced or utilized in any form or by any electronic,
mechanical, or other means, now known or hereafter
invented, including photocopying and recording, or in any
information storage or retrieval system, without permission
in writing from the publishers.

Trademark notice: Product or corporate names may be
trademarks or registered trademarks, and are used only for
identification and explanation without intent to infringe.

Library of Congress Cataloging-in-Publication Data
Steinberg, David I., author
Lead like the legends: advice and inspiration for teachers
and administrators/by David I. Steinberg
New York: Routledge, 2016. Includes bibliographical
references
LCCN 2015028268 ISBN 9781138948648 (hardback)
ISBN 9781138948655 (pbk.) ISBN 9781315669533 (e-book)
LCSH: Educational leadership. Teaching. School
management and organization
LCC LB2805 .S7456 2016 DDC 371.2–dc23
LC record available at http://lccn.loc.gov/2015028268

ISBN: 978-1-138-94864-8 (hbk)
ISBN: 978-1-138-94865-5 (pbk)
ISBN: 978-1-315-66953-3 (ebk)

Typeset in Palatino
by Florence Production Ltd, Stoodleigh, Devon, UK

Printed and bound in the United States of America by Publishers Graphics,
LLC on sustainably sourced paper.

I've been lucky! I have worked with thousands of inspiring teachers, principals, and others in schools all over the country who have taught me the life lessons in this book. I had a mother who taught me to love music and a father who taught me that nothing is as important as teaching others. I married a woman who shares all the same values and dreams, and our sons taught us how to put these lessons into action. This book is dedicated to them all.

Contents

About the Author   ix
Acknowledgments   xi
Prelude   xiii
How to Read *Lead Like the Legends*   xix

Legend: Judy Garland
LESSON 1   **BE SINCERE**   1

Legend: Rodgers and Hammerstein/Joe Raposo
LESSON 2   **BE OPTIMISTIC**   11

Legend: Ray Charles
LESSON 3   **ACCEPT NO LIMITS**   27

Legend: George Gershwin
LESSON 4   **BE ECLECTIC**   37

Legend: Duke Ellington
LESSON 5   **LEAD BY PARTICIPATING**   49

Legend: Leonard Bernstein
LESSON 6   **LEAD WITH IMAGINATION**   61

Legend: Marian Anderson
LESSON 7   **BE STRONG BY BEING PRINCIPLED**   73

Legend: Frank Sinatra
LESSON 8   **TRAIN TO GROW**   83

Legend: Bob Dylan
LESSON 9   **PUT THE MESSAGE ACROSS**   97

Legend: **Elvis Presley**
LESSON 10   **BE DARING AND HIGH ENERGY**   **107**

Legend: **Carlos Santana**
LESSON 11   **UNIFY**   **123**

Legend: **The Beatles**
LESSON 12   **USE TEAMWORK**   **135**

Legend: **The Temptations**
LESSON 13   **MOVE TOGETHER**   **149**

Legend: **Louis Armstrong**
LESSON 14   **BE YOURSELF**   **159**

Coda   173
Share Your Legends   177
Testimonials   178

About the Author

Dr. David Steinberg has taught the lessons of leadership to thousands of people in the United States and from around the world. He has had the unusual experience of having served as principal of all three levels of school (elementary, middle, and high school), with a record of having led each school to a significant rise in academic achievement and improvement in school climate. Previously, he taught almost all grade levels, including primary-aged students with multiple handicapping conditions, middle-school gifted students, and high-school students with learning disabilities.

He earned a B.S. in Political Science, History, and Elementary Education from the State University of New York at Brockport, an M.Ed. in Special Education from American University, and a Ph.D. in Education, Policy, Planning, and Administration from the University of Maryland.

Dr. Steinberg has been a keynote speaker and workshop leader at many conferences and has consulted with public school systems, private schools, colleges, and universities. He is Director of the Department of Professional Growth Systems with Montgomery County Public Schools in Maryland. He has taught graduate courses in Curriculum Theory, Instructional Supervision, Administration and Educational Research at Johns Hopkins University, Bowie State University, University of Maryland, and Hood College as well as undergraduate courses in Foundations of Education and Secondary Methods at Marymount University and Montgomery College.

Dr. Steinberg has won awards for teaching, school leadership, and building parent, business, and community partnerships including the Washington Post Distinguished Educational Leadership Award, Principal of the Year (Montgomery County Region of the Maryland Association of Student Councils), Outstanding

Citizen Award (Greater Gaithersburg Chamber of Commerce), Leadership Excellence Award (Division of Career and Technology Education), and the PTA Honorary Life Membership Award (Montgomery County Council of PTAs).

Dr. Steinberg's love of teaching is rivaled only by his love for music.

Acknowledgments

My wife, Joanie Steinberg, observed the presentation that was the catalyst for this book hundreds of times, and made countless indispensable improvements to it. She also edited every chapter with a keen eye to both the clarity of the messages as well as the underlying human meaning of each lesson. Like everything else in my life, she made it so much better.

Our sons, Dan and Ben, allowed their father to tell stories about them to audiences all around the country and graciously gave their permission to include them in this book.

My father, Harry Steinberg, modeled what a teacher can be and that a Renaissance man can have wide-ranging interests and integrate them into his life and work. My mother insisted that making and appreciating music is available to everyone, and that within everyone there is a song to share.

The inspiring teachers, administrators, and other staff members who devoted their professional lives to their students are the reason this book was written. When I contacted each of them whose stories I recounted, they responded with great generosity and humility, always genuinely surprised that they were being remembered as people who had left their mark on so many—and in my memory.

Prelude

This is a book about leadership and how the great musical legends can inspire us to lead our schools, classrooms, teams, businesses, organizations, and lives successfully. Although it may seem surprising that these leadership principles derive from the lives and work of songwriters, singers, and musicians, all the lessons are supported by the best research in education, psychology, management, and leadership.

The idea for this book came from an unusual request. Bob Hollinger, the energetic and elegantly dressed 90-year-old president of the local Kiwanis Club at the retirement community Leisure World, came into my principal's office at Magruder High School in Rockville, Maryland and asked me to deliver a speech on leadership that would appeal both to his senior citizen members and to our students in Key Club, the organization they sponsored. In the weeks leading up to the event, I couldn't think of a topic—especially one that would have some appeal to both 16- and 80-year-olds.

While listening to the radio, it occurred to me that there must be a few songs that everyone knows, songs such as: "Somewhere over the Rainbow," "Jailhouse Rock," "What a Wonderful World." But what possible leadership lessons could stem from such songs? Then I thought about Judy Garland's sincerity as she dreamed of a better place over the rainbow, Elvis Presley's high-energy performances, and the one and only Louis Armstrong's unique authenticity which came across in every song he played and sang.

To my great surprise, when I gave the speech and included the songs by playing them on a little upright piano, I could see that, no matter the age of the audience, there was something in these songs that moved them and brought back memories. The lessons we discussed from the performers' lives related

beautifully with the research on leadership and connected seamlessly to the character traits that Kiwanis, as a service organization, seeks to instill in the young people it mentors through Key
Club. There was something in this idea of connecting music and
research to leadership.

In the next few years, the idea took off and became a frequently
requested motivational speech (with accompanying music and
slides) for principals about how to lead their schools to attain
higher student achievement, while also fostering the kind of
supportive climate that parents would want their children to
experience. Before long it was adapted into a presentation for
teachers about how to become leaders in their classrooms so that
students are motivated to be part of a community in which
everyone feels that they are learning together. Then other groups
asked if the same leadership lessons would apply to their jobs.
For example, educational documentary television producers
found the lessons just as applicable to helping them lead their
staff. Soon it became a talk for school systems, boards of education, students, senior citizens, business leaders, directors of
non-profits, and others about how to lead their organizations and
lives by following the lessons taught to us by the great musical
legends and supported by the research.

I actually owe the concept behind this book to my mother.
Like all mothers, she wanted me to become a cultured person,
and made me take piano lessons when I was a kid growing up
in upstate New York. From sharing the ideas in this book with
thousands of people, I know that chances are, you—the reader—
either took music lessons, dance lessons, art lessons, or had tennis
or skating lessons or were coached in some other sport or activity,
because one of your parents or relatives thought it was a good
idea.

After taking classical piano lessons for a few months, I became
bored. It was the early 1960s. We were listening to the Beatles,
the Rolling Stones, Bob Dylan, Peter, Paul, and Mary. How was
I supposed to concentrate on Bach and Mozart? I wanted to quit.

However, my mother was smart, and like all mothers, smarter
than her children. She told the teacher, Mr. Sam Selig (who was
a part-time night club musician as well as a piano teacher), to

Here I am celebrating my birthday at the age when I took piano lessons. You know it's New York, because it's a birthday party in a diner.

teach me any type of music as long as I kept playing. So he taught me rock 'n roll. He showed me that rock was really built on the blues, and the blues is the basis for jazz. Before you knew it, I was playing popular songs and really getting into it.

A few years later, my next step was the same one taken by a lot of teenage boys. I started a garage band with my friends. Playing in a band was not only the key to being cool, but gave you a chance to talk to girls—especially if you weren't popular or on the basketball team. It was the 1960s, the age of flower power, and it doesn't get any more psychedelic than this—we named our band "The Underground Rainbow." We did a mean cover of the Doors' "Light My Fire" and played the only 20 songs we knew at school dances and hotel teen party rooms. I was the cool dude in the Nehru shirt and bell bottoms playing the electric piano and singing back-up. ("G-L-O-R-I-A. GLOOOOOO-RIAAAAA!") Never heard of us? Well, hardly anyone else has either.

I said goodbye to my dreams of touring the country playing rock 'n roll and I went to college. I became a teacher like my father who was a beloved third-grade teacher in our little town of Monticello in the Catskill Mountains of New York. I'm sure

Here is the teenage musician who couldn't decide if he wanted to be the next Bob Dylan or John Lennon.

I became a teacher because of him. I saw the kids in town talk to him and ask his advice, even years after he had them as students. He always said there was nothing better you could do with your life, no greater contribution you could make to society, and no greater satisfaction that you could experience than by becoming a teacher.

When I began teaching I found it hard to stretch my paycheck, so to pay the bills I began playing piano for weddings, bar mitzvahs, and anniversary parties. I still play a mean "New York, New York"—the song most requested after everyone has had a few drinks. Although I loved being a teacher, I secretly still wanted to be a musician in a Manhattan hotel café, playing sophisticated Broadway show tunes by George Gershwin and jazz standards by Duke Ellington. All the while I was spending nights moonlighting, during my day job I was watching the more experienced teachers, as new teachers do, and I found many role models. I spent time thinking about what they were doing and I especially took note of what seemed to work to make their classrooms good places for students to learn.

After teaching for about ten years, I became a principal, first of an elementary school, then of a middle school, and later of a high school. I was still listening to a lot of my musical heroes, and at the same time I was watching my co-workers. There were principals I admired who were doing great things—really moving their schools ahead. There were teachers I observed who had extraordinary skills, not only with their students but by influencing other teachers as well. There were central office administrators who were so knowledgeable and helpful. There were support staff, like teacher assistants, secretaries, and bus drivers, who often weren't credited but were sometimes making the biggest differences in children's lives.

Soon I started seeing connections. There were ideas I could learn about leadership from my favorite songwriters, musicians, and singers, and these same strategies were being used with excellent results by the school leaders I admired. To my surprise, when I began studying leadership as I worked on my Ph.D. at the University of Maryland, I found the ideas aligned with the research-based practices in the wealth of available literature on leadership in business, education, government, and the military.

As a result, the ideas in this book are fully supported, research-based strategies, but shared in a way that people have found to be user-friendly because they are connected to something we all love—music and the people who make it.

The lessons are told through stories of real leaders, drawn mainly from the world of schools where I've spent my entire working life. All of the stories are true, recorded here to the best of my memory. But to check that I got them right, I played internet detective and searched until I found each person profiled. Some of them I hadn't been in touch with for many years and many had moved to other parts of the country. In each case, they generously gave me permission to share these events with you. They are stories that we can all take to heart, no matter the type of organizations we want to successfully lead or the meaningful lives we want for ourselves. I hope they inspire you as they have inspired me.

Now let's explore the question that this book seeks to answer: what can we learn about leadership from the legends of music, from the research, and from extraordinary people, in order to enrich our work and our lives?

How to Read
Lead Like the Legends

What can we learn about leading our classrooms, schools, teams, businesses, organizations, and our own lives from the legends of music?

The chapters in this book can be read in any order. Although there is an intended progression in the leadership lessons, from individual characteristics to strategies for working with others in teams, departments, or organizations as a whole, what's most important is to spend time reflecting on how the lessons apply to your own life and work.

Each chapter begins by introducing a musical legend. You can go to iTunes, Amazon, YouTube, or any other online source to hear them. I suggest listening to the songs as you begin to read a chapter to help you associate the music with your learning. Then listen again afterwards, to give yourself time to think about how the ideas in the chapter connect to the music and to your own thoughts and feelings. A section following each chapter is provided for you to record your reflections—especially ideas about the important people in your life who exemplify similar traits—as well as your own personal commitments to apply the leadership lessons in whatever areas of your life in which you will become a legendary leader.

Judy Garland

LESSON 1:
Be Sincere

Judy Garland in The Wizard of Oz
Credit: MGM/Photofest ©MGM

WHEN JUDY GARLAND is singing "Somewhere Over the Rainbow," it fills us all with childhood memories of the magic of *The Wizard of Oz*.

Do you think she was beautiful?

Certainly she wasn't sexy like Marilyn Monroe or beautiful like any of today's hot stars. She was a girl named Frances Gumm from Grand Rapids, Minnesota—one of the singing Gumm Sisters. She had a girl-next-door kind of quality, and she didn't think she was attractive at all.

Yet, it's undeniable that she does have a kind of beauty. Where does that beauty come from? It isn't only physical. Something happens to us when she sings. At the beginning of the movie, when it's still in black and white, and Dorothy is still in Kansas, and she sings that lovely song, don't we all believe that she knows, in her heart, that there is a better place somewhere over the rainbow? We are absolutely sure she believes it. In other words, she's sincere.

That is the first leadership lesson of *Lead Like the Legends*:

BE SINCERE

The Lesson Goes to School:
How Educators Can Be Sincere

In the 1990s, the city of Gaithersburg, in central Maryland, wanted to tear down the Lee Street apartments. If you got off the commuter train in the center of town and walked two blocks downhill on Summit Avenue, you might think you were in a slum, rather than in a booming, Washington, D.C. suburban bedroom community—not at all the image of revitalization that the city council wanted to present to the world. The home-grown mayor, Ed Bohrer, was an astute political leader and very sensitive to his community. He called a meeting of the three principals whose schools had students living in the apartments. I was the middle-school principal. He told us that he wanted us to contact every family. If they wanted their children to continue attending their neighborhood schools, the city would arrange for them to move, at no cost, to another apartment nearby, without increasing their rent. He wanted to minimize the disruption to their lives, and he felt that we could help.

I went back to my office and wrote a letter to every family. It was a pseudo-personalized letter, the kind that we have all received from corporations, credit card companies, and charities. It was individually addressed to every family, but other than that, each one received the identical letter. I told them what the mayor said and offered to meet with them if they needed my assistance. I thought I had done a good job of reaching out to the families.

However, Sharon Jones, the principal of Gaithersburg Elementary School, did better. Sharon and her school counselor went to the Lee Street apartments and knocked on every door to ask whether there were any school-aged children living there, and then personally offered to help the family if they wanted their child to stay at her school. After you meet a principal who does something like that, who so sincerely cares about your children, who wouldn't want them to stay enrolled in that school?

That's what a sincere educator does—she does it personally, because that's what schools (or any organizations) are when they are at their best: a personal experience, where everyone is treated as a valued individual.

The way Sharon Jones acted (and the mayor, too) is a com-bination of two qualities—sincerity merged with effectiveness (carefully planning and carrying out a job). The syndicated columnist and presidential speechwriter Peggy Noonan put it like this: "Sincerity and competence is a strong combination. In politics, it is everything."[1] These two leadership characteristics are essential for every type of work and every goal we hope to accomplish in our lives. Denise Schaefer combined these two traits to turn a high-school graduation into a moment that no one who was there will ever forget.

A graduation coordinator is a thankless job, and we felt very grateful that Denise volunteered to take on this huge and complicated task at our school, Colonel Zadok Magruder High School, in Rockville, Maryland. Mobilizing hundreds of high-school seniors and the entire faculty and staff, coordinating the program and its many participants, and dealing sensitively with the requests of parents and other relatives—all of this would be overwhelming to most people. Yet Denise ran some of the most well-organized and highly regarded commencement ceremonies anyone in Montgomery County had ever seen. She did all of this with proactive and detailed planning, close collaboration with everyone, and a willingness to meet the needs of every student. She felt we owed that high level of service and respect to all of our graduates and their families. I will always remember this example of Denise's sincere thoughtfulness.

Ryan was a student with congenital muscular dystrophy, which caused such severe physical disabilities that he only had the mobility to slightly move one of his hands, which he used to work the toggle switch to drive his heavy, motorized wheelchair. He had excelled in his four years of high school despite several lengthy hospitalizations. Denise was going to make sure that Ryan had a graduation like all of his other classmates, or what we now call a fully inclusive experience, and to accomplish this goal she went far beyond the extra mile.

Months before the ceremony, Denise met with Ryan and his mother so that she would better understand his needs. She talked with the special education teacher and counselor who managed his case and the paraeducator who assisted him through his school day. Next she went downtown to D.A.R. Constitution Hall, where graduation would be held, to look for ways that Ryan could participate, along with everyone else, in every part of the ceremony. She mapped out where he would sit, the path he would travel to the stage, how he would return to his seat— all with a view to making his experience as similar as possible to every other senior's.

In June, we held our graduation rehearsal in the gym, a long and challenging process in itself; by late spring, seniors think they are finished with high school, and the last thing they want to do is sit in a hot gymnasium practicing how to receive their diploma and shake hands with the principal and superintendent. Usually it's hard enough to get them to be quiet and listen to directions, but it was obvious to everyone that Ms. Schaefer was doing something very unusual. She was briefing the staff volunteers and student ushers so that Ryan would have a rehearsal experience that would make him feel comfortable and prepare him for how to navigate the actual layout of Constitution Hall. Denise was now walking alongside Ryan on a long, masking-taped, marked pathway around the gym so that they would know exactly what to do on the big day. When the seniors saw this happening, they became unusually quiet. A teacher was making a special effort for a student and, in that moment, the hush that fell over the room demonstrated their respect for what she was doing.

I have purposely described this example in great detail, because I want to emphasize the extraordinary lengths to which Denise had gone in order to make graduation an unforgettable memory for Ryan, his family, and friends. A few minutes before his name was called, student ushers silently assumed their stations and Ryan started his journey that had been meticulously planned by Ms. Schaefer: through the auditorium aisles, out to the hallway, just like the masking-taped pathway in the gym, then up a ramp and behind the curtain. At last, when the students whose last names began with T, U, and V were finished receiving their diplomas, the senior class sponsor announced "Ryan Walsh" and, with his usual determined look in his eyes and without hesitation, he proudly wheeled across the stage, in line in the exact right place alphabetically, to receive his diploma. There wasn't a dry eye in the house. In fact, there was a spontaneous standing ovation led by students and parents, which lasted until he left the stage as he had entered, confident and happy—an emotional and unforgettable moment for everyone.

In addition to competence, sincerity has to be supported by one other irreplaceable requirement—empathy. Daniel Goleman, the author of the best-selling book *Emotional Intelligence*,[2] describes the characteristic this way: "Emotional intelligence—which refers to how you handle your own feelings, how well you empathize and get along with other people—is just a key human skill."[3] Jerry Perlet, principal of Sherwood Elementary School in Sandy Spring, Maryland, knew how to put that unbeatable combination of empathy plus sincerity and competence to work for children.

The first day of kindergarten can be pretty scary to a five-year-old. I remember crying on my first day until my mother sat me next to Karen, a cute, freckle-faced girl I knew from preschool. I wasn't surprised to hear that Jerry was faced with a similar situation.

On the first day of kindergarten, like many parents who want to ensure their children get off to a good start, Roberto's parents brought him to school. They introduced him to his teacher, stood in the back of the room for a little while, and when they were sure he was comfortable they went to work. Jerry was the type of principal who knew every child by name. Every year, on the first day of school, he spent time in the kindergarten classes, getting to know his newest students. He'd sit on the rug with them and follow along with the teacher's directions. It didn't take long for the girls and boys to realize that their bald, six-foot, ever-smiling principal with the Mickey Mouse tie was a warm, friendly man who they could trust.

On the way home though, Roberto took the school bus. It was noisy and there were older kids who he didn't know. He wasn't sure where to sit, and when he finally found a seat, he couldn't see over the green high-backed seats; although he heard a lot of kids talking and laughing, he couldn't see or hear well enough to join in. He felt very much alone.

The next morning Roberto refused to go to school. His parents were confused. He seemed so happy when they watched him in the classroom yesterday, but Roberto couldn't explain his feelings. Even though his mother walked him to the bus stop and held his hand, when the bus arrived, he wouldn't get on. Roberto's parents went to see Mr. Perlet. Maybe the principal would have some ideas.

The next morning, Roberto stood at the bus stop, tightly gripping his mother's hand. When the bus pulled up to the curb, the other kids got on. Then something surprising happened. Roberto's principal, the tall, bald, smiling man with the Mickey Mouse tie, got off the bus. He crouched down real low so he would be about the same size as the scared little boy. Mr. Perlet put out his hand saying, "Roberto, let's go to school. It'll be fun!" Roberto exchanged his mother's hand for his principal's, and together they got on the bus. Sitting side by side, they waved at Roberto's mother, smiling and talking about what a great time they were going to have in kindergarten that day.

Roberto's parents never forgot what Jerry Perlet did that day. They even wrote a letter to the superintendent who told the story to all of the principals in the county, as a way of saying: This is what a great principal is—a human being who can feel what children feel and then reach out a hand to help them. Jerry

Perlet has empathy, or what Daniel Goleman calls emotional intelligence. Add it to competence—Jerry's knowledge of what needed to happen next—riding the bus to personally invite Roberto to come to school with him. Then merge both of these qualities of empathy and competence with sincerity—the sincere desire to help one little boy to not be afraid, but to come to school with confidence—and you have true leadership at its best.

You cannot move forward as a leader without a high level of commitment to the people you serve. Sincerity in leadership is all about the way Sharon Jones knocked on every apartment door to offer her help to displaced families; the way Denise Schaefer coordinated graduation so that a boy with a physical disability could fully participate; and the way Jerry Perlet offered his hand to a frightened kindergartener.

Confucius, China's most famous philosopher, said, "Sincerity and truth are the basis of every virtue."[4] We begin our learning about leadership here, because a sincere belief in serving others is the prerequisite and foundation for all the lessons which follow.

BE SINCERE is our first leadership lesson.

Notes

1   *Qualifications: Webster's Quotations, Facts and Phrases.* 2008. ICON Group International. San Diego, CA. P. 1.
2   Goleman, Daniel. 1995. *Emotional Intelligence.* Random House. New York.
3   See http://www.edutopia.org/daniel-goleman-emotional-intelligence.
4   See http://thinkexist.com/quotation/sincerity_and_truth_are_the_basis_of_every_virtue/252575.html.
5   Gibran, Kahlil, in Van Ekeren, Glenn. 1988. *Words for All Occasions.* Prentice Hall. Englewood Cliffs, NJ.

Reflection Activity 1

It is well to give when asked, but it is better to give unasked, through understanding.[5]

Kahlil Gibran, artist, poet, and writer

What an encouraging feeling when someone tells you that your work, your future, your life really matters! According to Daniel Goleman, the "key human skill" of empathy can make a person feel supported in facing life's challenges. Principal Sharon Jones empathized with the families moving out of their soon-to-be-demolished apartments and wanted to help them, graduation coordinator Denise Schaefer felt that Ryan would want to experience the ceremony in the same way as every other senior, and principal Jerry Perlet understood why a frightened kindergartener wouldn't want to get on the school bus. They gave the "better" way, as the poet said, "unasked."

As you complete the first reflection activity, begin by thinking about these examples and then by remembering who has made a meaningful difference in your life. In what ways did they sincerely communicate their belief in you?

In your life and work, who has demonstrated **Leadership Lesson 1: Be Sincere**? What did they do and say? Be as specific as possible. What did you learn from them that you want to apply to your own life and work?

_____

_____

_____

_____

_____

_____

_____

_____

_____

_____

_____

_____

_____

_____

_____

Reflect further by doing the self-rating scales below. If this leadership lesson is one you have just started using, you are at the beginning phase. If you are using this leadership lesson regularly, you are now at the practicing phase. Like expert musicians we need to commit to practicing these lessons for our entire careers and lives. When you have mastered this leadership lesson and incorporated it naturally into your repertoire, you have reached the leading level.

Rate yourself using this scale. Mark a place on the line that represents _your_ current state on **Leadership Lesson 1: Be Sincere.**

1	2	3	4	5

| Beginning | | Practicing | | Leading |

Rate your team, department, school, office, business, or organization using this scale. Mark a place on the line that represents _your group_'s current state on **Leadership Lesson 1: Be Sincere.**

1	2	3	4	5

| Beginning | | Practicing | | Leading |

What commitment will you and the people with whom you work make to fulfill this leadership characteristic? How can you incorporate the **leadership lesson of being sincere** into your life and work? What concrete action steps will you take? What will be the sequence? What timeline will you follow?

Commitment:

_____

_____

_____

_____

_____

_____

Action Steps	Person(s) Responsible	Timeline

Rodgers and Hammerstein/ Joe Raposo

LESSON 2:
Be Optimistic

Richard Rodgers and Oscar Hammerstein
Credit: Photofest

Joe Raposo
Credit: Photofest

"OH WHAT A BEAUTIFUL MORNING" is the opening song from the groundbreaking Broadway musical *Oklahoma!*[1] When Curly the cowboy rides through the field, with the sun shining above him, singing "the corn is as high as an elephant's eye," you know that he is going to have a wonderful day.

If you've seen the musical *The King and I*, you'll certainly remember these songs: "Getting to Know You" and "I Whistle a Happy Tune."[2] Even when Anna the school teacher is anxious about her new life in Siam, she teaches her son to "whistle a happy tune," and when she meets her students, she is looking forward to "getting to know all about" them.

Hearing the songs of Richard Rodgers and Oscar Hammerstein, you feel their positive view of life, and that is the lesson we can learn from these great American show-tune songwriters:

BE OPTIMISTIC

We are all attracted to a positive belief in the future. Successful presidential candidates always use this idea in their campaigns. Ronald Reagan's "Morning in America" defeated a sitting president, Jimmy Carter, who talked realistically, but depressingly, about our "National Malaise." A few years later, the candidates for president and vice-president, Bill Clinton and Al Gore, envisioned building a "Bridge to Tomorrow" and unseated the first President Bush, even though many people seemed to think the state of the country was relatively healthy. Barack Obama became president in 2008 with a theme of "Change You Can Believe In," which promised a better future, and a slogan of "Yes We Can," which communicated our ability to make it happen.

Do you remember the theme song from the world's most popular and successful children's television show—*Sesame Street*?[3] What kind of day is it going to be on Sesame Street? You, of course, immediately think: "A sunny day," just like the song says.

The composer was Joe Raposo, who not only wrote the show's theme song,[4] but also such memorable lyrics as Kermit's song, "It's not easy bein' green."[5] He left a legacy of so many wonderful songs for Children's Television Workshop.[6]

When our two sons, Daniel and Benjamin, were preschoolers and heard the *Sesame Street* theme song on TV, they would run like sprinters, from wherever they were in the house, to magically appear in the living room to watch the show. When young children hear those bouncy

Sesame Street *cast*
Credit: PBS/Photofest ©PBS

beginning chords, they just know that their friends Bert, Ernie, Big Bird, and Elmo are going to have a great day on *Sesame Street*—and they are, too.

The Lesson Goes to School: How Educators Can Be Optimistic

The lesson from many of Rodgers and Hammerstein's songs and the *Sesame Street* theme song is **Be Optimistic**. I'm not talking about a starry-eyed, rose-colored glasses, unrealistic optimism, but rather a faith that today and tomorrow are going to be happy, satisfying, and productive. It's a combination of confidence and hope, looking forward to an even better future, and working hard to take us there—or at least move us in that direction.

In every school that has ever succeeded, there was this type of pervasive belief that the students could and would achieve and that the climate would get better.

My first principalship was of the small, old, red-brick Rosemont Elementary School in Gaithersburg, Maryland. Ann Meyer, my supervisor, the straight-talking and insightful community superintendent, called me into her office to give me what she called her "charge"—my focus as the new principal. The situation she described really struck me with its depth of understanding and stuck with me throughout the years I worked there.

She said, "The people in that little school have been watching new, big, modern schools being built all around them. They feel forgotten. Show them you believe in that little school and in them and their future."

I went to work the next day and decided to meet the staff and parents to hear their opinions about the state of the school. After listening to them for a little while, I realized she had nailed it— that was exactly how they felt; that no one in the school system noticed or cared about them. I knew that should be my mission, to help everyone believe that we would become a great school, a place where everybody would want to send their children.

Each year we planned activities to proclaim proudly that we knew we could be a great school. We started a cutting-edge program to teach thinking strategies so that our students could do higher-level work; we installed ceiling fans (because our old building didn't have air conditioning) to provide some relief from the infamous Washington area heat and humidity; we began a business/school partnership with the local mall to provide kids with incentives and opportunities for good citizenship and academic performance; and we built a float, formed a parent/staff band, and marched with our students in the town's Labor Day parade. (We won the award for best elementary school spirit, and even though we were the only elementary school in the parade, we displayed the trophy, with pride, in the main office.) The message was clear: we would do whatever it took, because we knew we could be a wonderful school, even if we had to take many of the steps ourselves to make sure it happened.

It did happen and then some! Achievement went up and parents no longer talked about transferring their children to surrounding schools. Why would you leave a school with such a positive, sunny spirit? Optimism and momentum attract.

I'm certainly not sharing the story of the Rosemont turnaround to say that effective teaching and management are not important, or that hard work, sweat, and tears are not essential to a school's progress—they are. The moral of the story, though, is that none of these things would have been enough in themselves. The powerful catalyst of optimism, an underlying belief in our success, was the essential basic ingredient.

Years before becoming an administrator, I worked for the Department of Title I (the federal education program serving high-poverty schools) as a teacher specialist responsible for insuring the program was serving the students in greatest need. One of my first tasks was to call each elementary principal in my area to schedule a get-to-know-each-other meeting. I started calling the principals and, as expected, all I managed to accomplish was scheduling the meetings through their secretaries.

However, when I called Viers Mill Elementary in Rockville, the principal, John Burley, answered the phone. I told him who I was and why I wanted to meet with him. He surprised me by saying, "Do you know anything about cooperative learning?" I said I knew a little. He quickly replied, "Great! We're having lunch in an hour to plan a staff in-service. How about joining us?" In an hour, not only was I at the school having lunch with the staff, but I was on the planning team. In the next hour, I found myself volunteering to be a co-presenter for the workshop. I couldn't help myself; I wanted to work with these friendly people who so readily included a newcomer. As a result, I got to know the staff faster and better than in any other school where I was assigned that year. Whenever I had a little unscheduled time, I found myself over there helping out—covering a class, doing an in-service, working out a testing problem, meeting with a parent, or training a teacher and paraeducator (teaching assistant) to plan and work together as a team.

I thought about that principal and asked myself: "How did John do it?" "How did he get me involved and contributing so quickly and effectively?" He did it through optimism. He didn't know me when I called him. He didn't know if I could be of any help or if I was just a central office bureaucrat who wanted to walk him through the required red tape to get the Title I funding he needed for his school. Yet instead of answering my call in a coolly impersonal manner, he put out a hopeful feeler: "Do you know anything about cooperative learning?" Then he cheerfully offered an invitation, "How about joining us?" So upbeat, so inviting, such a positive belief that someone you don't even know might be able to be part of the team. That's leadership through optimism.

A teacher who is optimistic can change the climate of an entire classroom, and in so doing can change children's lives forever. Ann Pokoyk was that kind of teacher. She was the first teacher I ever hired; she already had over 30 years of experience.

I was spending as much time as I could at Viers Mill Elementary School because John and his staff made me feel so welcome. One day I was asked to substitute for a fifth-grade class because the teacher was out sick. I remember what we did to make substitutes' lives a living hell when I was a kid, so I was very surprised to find a class of the best-behaved, most helpful students you could ever imagine. They showed me how the teacher took attendance, where she kept her lesson plans and materials, and gave me a briefing on the classroom's daily procedures. It was a remarkably friendly, cooperative atmosphere. The teacher, Ann Pokoyk, had already been teaching for over 25 years, but it was obvious that it took more than mere longevity to lead such a delightful and respectful classroom. Ann was the type of person who liked and believed in her students; only children who were treated this way would, in turn, treat a substitute with such kindness and consideration. Once I got to know her, I vowed that if ever I became a principal I would actively recruit Ann Pokoyk.

On my first day on the job as a principal, I was told I needed to hire a teacher. Not just any teacher but a teacher for the third-/fourth-grade combination class. The enrollment numbers had resulted in the need for one class that was made up of half third graders and half fourth graders. This was a problem. Not for the kids, but for their parents. Most parents believe that if their child is in either half of a combination class, they are going to be cheated out of the teacher's full attention, since the teacher has to split her time between two curriculums and two age groups.

It isn't true. If you take any class of students, all supposedly of the same age and in the same grade level, there are going to be enormous differences in their skills and abilities. In fact, there is going to be such a wide range in achievement that it is going to encompass several grade levels. Most fourth-grade classes will have some kids reading at the first-grade level and some already reading at the middle- or high-school level. This is typical. In part, that explains why teaching is such a challenging profession. Every child is a mixture of strengths and weaknesses. You take that pattern and apply it to a class of 25 and you have complexity to the 25th power. That represents a lot of different needs.

The influential educator Madeline Hunter[7] used to say that teaching is all about decision making and that a teacher makes literally thousands of decisions every day. This partially explains why teachers are so tired at the end of the day. It also explains the answer to the old question: who are the only people who think teaching is easy? People who have never taught.

To my great relief, Ann agreed to take the job of teaching the third- and fourth-grade combination class. The kids immediately fell in love with her. Next came the big test—Back-to-School Night. This is actually a new principal's first big exam. On their way out to the parking lot at the end of the evening, the parents stop by the main office and tell the principal if the teachers and the school look first-rate or if there is anything wrong. The principal is a little like a producer on the opening night of a Broadway show, and after the closing curtain, hears the critics' reviews. At the end of that evening, when the parents came out of Ms. Pokoyk's class and walked by the office to tell me their thoughts, it was clear that they didn't care what we called the class or what grade levels it contained, as long as this wonderful woman was their children's teacher.

The moment that defines Ann Pokoyk's optimistic approach with all her students might seem a little strange, because it was the kind of incident in which everything might have gone wrong. Here is what happened.

The following year we had a challenging class of sixth graders that needed a teacher. They were far below level in their reading and math skills, and some of them had a history of behavior problems. Some had learning disabilities and some were new immigrants with their English-language skills needing a lot of improvement. The only consolation I could offer to a teacher for agreeing to take this class was a slightly reduced class size— 20 students instead of the usual 25. But let's face it; 20 needy kids take much more energy than a larger class of average or above-average students. Thank goodness Ann agreed to take the class. Just as she had with taking on the combination class the year before, she approached this new assignment with a full heart. She embraced the sixth-grade students as hers. While she firmly insisted they do all their classwork and homework completely, giving it their best effort, she told them how much she enjoyed working with them and how much she believed in them.

The moment that I remember vividly happened one day when I was walking from class to class, taking a quick look around the school at how teachers and students were doing. I have always been a believer in the strategy usually attributed to executives at the company Hewlett-Packard, that some call "management by wandering (or walking) around."[8] I think there are two kinds of principals (or two kinds of managers in any organization): the ones who sit in their offices and the ones who walk their buildings to see, first-hand, the kinds of teaching and learning taking place. You can learn a lot by analyzing the data on your computer screen, but it doesn't take the place of being where the real day-to-day work is happening.

On that day, I walked into Ann's room and saw a few students gathered around a table with Ann discussing their reading and writing. The rest of the class was working independently and quietly. As usual, everything looked good in Ann Pokoyk's classroom; everyone was learning. I turned around to leave. As I began to walk out through the door, I heard a loud CRASH! I quickly turned back and here is what I saw: Ms. Pokoyk was on the floor, flat on her back, with the table on top of her. It was a flimsy table and the legs must have given way. She had landed on the hard linoleum floor with her chair tipped over backwards, books and papers strewn all over the place.

That's when I saw an amazing turn of events. Or maybe I should say that's when I both saw and didn't see it. In an average class of 11- and 12-year-olds, if their teacher falls over with a crash, like in a pratfall, you would hear plenty of laughter. "Oh, that is so funny!" they'd shout. "Did you see that?" they'd ask each other, replaying it, imitating it, enjoying the moment, as if on instant replay, again and again. There would be pointing and hooting and hollering.

That was only one part of the surprising thing—what didn't happen. What did happen was even more amazing, and really touching. Every student jumped up and ran toward their teacher. Bending over her and reaching out to her, they were anxiously asking, "Ms. Pokoyk? Ms. Pokoyk, are you alright? Ms. Pokoyk?" They were so worried about her. They didn't want their beloved teacher to be hurt. They didn't want her to ever leave them. They cared about her because she cared about them. She believed in their goodness and, in that moment, their goodness was displayed clear as day. That is the power of an optimistic teacher who begins every year believing that her students can succeed and that she will not only be able to teach them, but she will also come to love them.

Everyone who studies education is introduced to the research on expectations. It has become accepted wisdom that the key to raising student achievement is high expectations. Education leaders constantly say it, and teachers hear it all the time. The most famous study on expectations took place in the 1960s when Lenore Jacobson, a principal from San Francisco, read a paper published in the *American Scientist* by Robert Rosenthal, a professor in the Department of Psychology and Social Relations at Harvard University. He had summarized evidence that the expectations of researchers might affect the responses of their subjects when carrying out psychological experiments. He also thought teachers' expectations for their students' intellectual performance might affect students' performance in the same way—a type of self-fulfilling prophecy. Ms. Jacobson wrote to

Dr. Rosenthal. If he was serious about doing an experiment with teachers, she would volunteer her school.

Their collaborative research, *Pygmalion in the Classroom*,[9] described what happened when teachers were told some of their students were about to intellectually blossom. What the teachers didn't know was that the students had been randomly selected so that there was, in fact, no evidence that the selected children were any more likely to significantly improve than any other students.

At the end of the year, the identified students did improve more than their peers. What could have caused this progress, if not the expectations that the teachers were somehow transmitting, through their own subtle and probably unconscious behaviors, to the children?

One inconsistency that Rosenthal and Jacobson found should be noted. The results were much more profound for the first- and second-grade students than for the students in the upper elementary grades. Some think this is because younger children are more susceptible to the power of their teachers' expectations. The older the children, the more established may be the teachers' views and the students' own views of their performance.

In the musical *My Fair Lady*,[10] the linguistics professor, Henry Higgins, expected the poor flower girl, Eliza Doolittle, to "become" a lady and so she did learn to speak and act like one. The teachers expected their students to "become" successful students, and they did achieve at much higher levels. We could predict that the next teachers who would have these students would begin the school year already believing they had more potential. After all, they had proven themselves. Having higher expectations for students not only provides them with a successful year in one teacher's classroom, but can set them up for future teachers to have the same high expectations.

Before teachers set high expectations for their students, they have to **BE OPTIMISTIC**. They need to believe that it is going to be a good day in their classrooms. It is going to be a day in which children learn. It is going to be a week, month, and year in which the children will achieve. Their students are going to go to middle school, high school, college, or other opportunities, and they are going to have exciting career options and make good choices about their futures. In other words, they see their students' potential for their entire lives, and they believe that, with hard work, they can reach their goals.

Just as a teacher can improve the lives of a classroom of children through optimism, a principal can influence an entire school in the same way.

"To Betty, there are no bad kids." That was how counselor Jeff Fahrner explained why he liked working at South Lake Elementary. Next door to an apartment complex and townhouses, across from the off-price shopping center, the school served kids from working- and middle-class families, and a large number of children whose families had few resources. When Betty Collins became South Lake's principal, a larger, newer school had been built nearby, and when the boundaries were redrawn, they siphoned off the kids living in the more expensive homes. With new families largely from Latin and South America moving in and the upper-middle class districted out, it was the time in a school's history that the writer Malcolm Gladwell would call a "tipping point,"[11] because it could start going downhill fast unless somebody did something to turn it around.

Betty Collins brought her sense of optimism to South Lake. Immediately, it was clear that she liked children. No, she loved children—all children. Maybe it had something to do with her personal history. Betty is African American and grew up in the county[12] in the 1950s and 1960s when it was completely segregated and as it gradually became desegregated. She wasn't going to ignore anyone or provide them with less encouragement because of their race, language, culture, or financial situation. She also wasn't going to focus on the issues that sometimes divide people. She was going to demonstrate through her own actions that she believed in everyone's potential—an optimism defined by her belief in people and what they are capable of doing.

I was lucky. Not only was Betty Collins our sons' principal, but when I became an elementary principal myself, she was assigned as my mentor. About once a month, we would walk through her school and talk about how she was trying to improve it and how I was trying to learn to improve mine. The memory of these walks through hallways and classrooms has always stayed with me. Children walked right up to Betty and threw their arms around her. The kindergarteners reached around her legs and the fifth graders put their arms around her waist. They wanted to touch her and feel the warmth of her hugs. It happened so often; I would hear a small voice say, "Mrs. Collins!" I knew right away two little arms were about to encircle her in a loving squeeze.

A few years later, the superintendent asked Betty to become principal of another school. She had done a great job bringing this community together on behalf of its children. Her favorite word was "together," and "Together we can make the difference" was her motto. She said and wrote it so often that it seemed natural that we should all believe it. How then was it possible that she would be leaving us? Adults understand the inevitability that talented administrators are asked to take other challenging assignments. Kids see it differently. Dan, our oldest son, a big, strong, and outwardly stoic boy, was in fourth grade when she made her announcement. He hadn't known any other principal. He cried when he heard her say she was leaving, and he wasn't alone. So many children cried and teachers were frantically calling the front office asking Betty to please come to their classrooms to put the children back "together."

Something happens when a leader is optimistic. Not just an optimism that a school's test scores will go up, or working conditions will improve, or productivity will rise; but a firm belief in every person's worth. Optimistic leaders live that belief by taking time with everyone who requires their help and supporting everyone who needs their guidance. They know something magical happens. People begin believing in themselves.

Notes

1 *Oklahoma!*, Richard Rodgers and Oscar Hammerstein II, copyright 1943, by Williamson Music.
2 *The King and I*, Richard Rodgers and Oscar Hammerstein II, copyright 1951, by Williamson Music.
3 Sesame Street Workshop and subsidiaries, http://www.sesame workshop.org.

4   *Sesame Street* theme, words by Bruce Hart, Jon Stone, and Joe Raposo, music by Joe Raposo, 1969, Sesame Street.

5   "Green (Bein' Green)," words and music by Joe Raposo, copyright 1970 and 1972, Jonico Music.

6   Former name of Sesame Workshop, formation 1969, 1 Lincoln Plaza, New York, 10023.

7   Hunter, Madeline. 1979. Teaching Is Decision Making. *Educational Leadership* 37(1): 62–5. Hunter, Madeline. 1982. *Mastery Teaching.* TIP Publications. El Segundo, CA.

8   Mears, Mike. 2009. *Leadership Elements: A Guide to Building Trust.* Google Books link: BooksG-TOC-51. P. 51. Peters, Tom and Waterman, Robert H. 1982. *In Search of Excellence.* Google Books link: BooksG-FOC-289. P. 289.

9   Rosenthal, R. and Jacobson, L. 1968. *Pygmalion in the Classroom: Teacher Expectation and Pupils' Intellectual Development.* Holt, Rinehart, and Winston. New York.

10   The musical *My Fair Lady* by Alan J. Lerner (lyrics) and Frederick Lowe (music) (1956) was based on the play *Pygmalion: A Romance in Five Acts* by George Bernard Shaw (1912), which in turn was based on the Greek myth about Pygmalion, a sculptor who wished his statue of an ideal woman would become real and whose prayers were eventually answered by the goddess Venus.

11   Gladwell, Malcolm. 2000. *The Tipping Point: How Little Things Can Make a Big Difference.* Little, Brown, and Company. Boston, MA.

12   Montgomery County, Maryland.

13   See http://en.wikipedia.org/wiki/Johann_Wolfgang_von_Goethe.

14   Shaw, Bernard. 1916. *Pygmalion.* Brentano. New York.

Reflection Activity 2

Treat people as if they were what they ought to be and you may help them to become what they are capable of being.[13]

Johann Wolfgang von Goethe,
German writer and poet

Whether you're listening to the songs of Rodgers and Hammerstein or your children are drawn to the *Sesame Street* theme song, there's a feeling of optimism in the air—the same climate that the extraordinary teacher Ann Pokoyk created in her classroom. She communicated to every child her complete belief in them and their potential, a real-life example of Rosenthal and Jacobson's *Pygmalion in the Classroom* experiment, but with the critical difference that Ann Pokoyk told *every* student, not just randomly selected lucky ones, that she expected them to blossom in her care. Principal Betty Collins, for whom there were "no bad kids," brought the same type of optimism to every child who attended and every adult who worked in her school. Together they did make a difference.

As you complete the reflection activity below, keep in mind the words of Eliza Doolittle, the flower girl who becomes transformed in George Bernard Shaw's play *Pygmalion* and in Lerner and Lowe's musical *My Fair Lady*. "The difference between a flower girl and a lady isn't how she behaves; it's how she is treated."[14]

In your life and work, who do you know who has demonstrated **Leadership Lesson 2: Be Optimistic**? What did they do and say? Be as specific as possible. What did you learn from them that you want to apply to your own life and work?

_____

_____

_____

_____

_____

_____

_____

_____

_____

_____

_____

_____

_____

_____

_____

_____

Reflect further by doing the self-rating scales below. If this leadership lesson is one you have just started using, you are at the beginning phase. If you are using this leadership lesson regularly, you are now at the practicing phase. Like expert musicians we need to commit to practicing these lessons for our entire careers and lives. When you have mastered this leadership lesson and incorporated it naturally into your repertoire, you have reached the leading level.

Rate yourself using this scale. Mark a place on the line that represents _your_ current state on **Leadership Lesson 2: Be Optimistic**.

1	2	3	4	5
Beginning		Practicing		Leading

Rate your team, department, school, office, business, or organization using this scale. Mark a place on the line that represents *your group*'s current state on **Leadership Lesson 2: Be Optimistic.**

1	2	3	4	5

Beginning	Practicing	Leading

What commitment will you and the people with whom you work make to fulfill this leadership characteristic? How can you incorporate the leadership lesson of **Being Optimistic** into your life and work? What concrete action steps will you take? What will be the sequence? What timeline will you follow?

Commitment:

_____

_____

_____

_____

_____

_____

Action Steps	Person(s) Responsible	Timeline

Ray Charles

LESSON 3:
Accept No Limits

Ray Charles
Credit: 20th Century Fox/Photofest © 20th Century Fox

NO ONE HAS EVER INTERPRETED a song like Ray Charles. His incredible talent is often referred to as the "genius of Ray Charles."

In addition to being blind and overcoming that physical disability, he surmounted the obstacles of poverty and discrimination to achieve greatness. He didn't accept those limits, nor did he allow anybody to limit him or his music.

There is a scene in the movie *Ray*[1] that takes place in a recording studio. At first, the camera is focused on Ray at a grand piano, with a chorus behind him and a full orchestra filling the room. He is recording the tender, sentimental, Hoagy Carmichael classic "Georgia on My Mind."[2] With the violins swelling, the song sounds lush—just like the recording. The camera pans to the control room where we see a discussion among the record executives who are saying that this will never work. It's such a big departure from his rhythm and blues songs like "I Got a Woman"[3] and "What'd I Say."[4] They are sure a sweet, plaintive ballad will never sell. Of course, they couldn't have been more wrong, and Ray couldn't have been more right. It became his biggest hit and is probably the one we now think of as his signature song. The same thing happened later when he decided to record country music because he liked the songs and the stories they told. The studio executives told him he couldn't do it. Again, he had to insist. He even had to quit his record label and sign a contract with another company. Again he was proven right, becoming the biggest country cross-over artist of all time.

This is the leadership lesson we can learn from Ray Charles:

ACCEPT NO LIMITS

The Lesson Goes to School:
How Educators Can Accept No Limits

When I think of someone who accepted no limits, I think about Brenda Robins, our sons' kindergarten teacher. Brenda was the embodiment of Albert Einstein's rule to live by: "In the middle of difficulty lies opportunity."[5] She was already the kind of kindergarten teacher parents hoped their children would have as their introduction to elementary school. But late in her career, she was diagnosed with multiple sclerosis (MS).

I'm not at all sure I would go on working with MS gradually taking away my independence. Brenda Robins, however, did not stop teaching until she felt she had no choice. My wife and I feel lucky that she was there to teach both our boys. By the time our older son, Dan, was in her class, sometimes she had to use a motorized wheelchair scooter to get around, and two years later, when our younger son, Ben, had her, she was completely dependent on it.

Instead of viewing that chair as a limitation, she used it as a teaching opportunity. Her kids would do anything to be hoisted up for a ride. Do you know how many books kindergarteners will read to be able to earn the most honored place to sit and read to their teacher? A lot.

The annual elementary school Halloween parade was even more special. Teachers led their classes around the school with everyone in costume, and you could always count on the more enthusiastic teachers to be wearing costumes, too. But Mrs. Robins had them all beat. She dressed up as a cowgirl and turned that motorized scooter into her horse. She led the parade all around the school. Every kid thought she was the coolest teacher they had ever seen. That is how we work beyond the roadblocks that life sometimes has a way of putting in our paths.

If Ray Charles and Brenda Robins could persevere and succeed by **Accepting No Limits**, so can we.

This lesson also applies to administrators and even entire schools. In 1997, Jamie Virga became the principal of Viers Mill Elementary School in Silver Spring, Maryland, just a few miles north of Washington, D.C.—a school with a very high poverty rate with over half the children qualifying for the federal free lunch program,[6] a very high mobility rate with families constantly moving into and out of the neighborhood, and a very high enrollment of students who were new immigrants (about one-third) from 42 countries who were just learning English. By most measures, it was a school that was only marginally succeeding.

During his eight years as principal, Jamie held fast to two beliefs: first, his students did not have to be limited by their circumstances, and second, he and the staff did not have to see themselves as limited by the challenging situation in which they found themselves. They believed the children could overcome the limits of poverty, mobility, and the need to learn a new language, and that they were the ones who were going to make these achievements possible. They had faith in their own ability to change things for the better.

In psychology, this is sometimes called "self-efficacy"—an idea originated by Canadian-born, Stanford University psychologist, Albert Bandura[7]—which says that, through reflection, we can have some control over our thoughts and feelings. If we can control our thoughts and feelings, we can also have some control over our motivation and eventually choose our actions. If we can determine our actions, we can alter our environments or improve our situations. We don't have to think of ourselves as at the mercy of environmental factors, the way B. F. Skinner[8] pictured us or at the mercy of inner impulses, the way Sigmund Freud[9] described us. Albert Bandura's idea was a huge shift, maintaining that we can be proactive; we can have some power over our own lives.

I once took a graduate course in personnel management at the University of Maryland. The professor, Dr. J. Edward Andrews, a former director of human resources for a large public school system, taught us a basic rule for recruiting and hiring good employees: "Past performance is the best predictor of future performance." He said: "You want to hire good teachers? Don't worry about IQ. Look at their college transcripts. Did they take higher-level challenging courses? Did they earn good grades? What you want are people who worked hard in college, because chances are, they will work hard in your job, too."

While it's probably true that a person's track record is a good way to predict how they will perform, does that have to be the end of the story? Is it always true that a person's past determines their future?

What's especially interesting about the theory of self-efficacy is that it says that people's beliefs about themselves and about their ability to change their situations can be even more powerful than their past performance. Beliefs can trump experience—an amazing thought!

We could say that your beliefs eventually determine whether your experiences will be successful. In the saying usually attributed to Mahatma Gandhi:[10]

Your beliefs become your thoughts,
Your thoughts become your words,
Your words become your actions,
Your actions become your habits,
Your habits become your values,
Your values become your destiny.

If a school has a past record of mediocre performance, but the staff change their thinking and begin to believe that they can turn things around, can their thoughts and the actions they take as a result of those thoughts change reality? What happened to Jamie Virga and the staff and students at Viers Mill Elementary? Did they succeed? Did they ever!

As a result of their hard work and their belief in their ability to take their students beyond the limits of their circumstances, Viers Mill Elementary School was named a Maryland Blue Ribbon School of Excellence in 2004. In 2005, they won the National Blue Ribbon. No small accomplishment, especially when you consider that the school won the recognition not only for its dramatic gains, but also for its academically superior achievement.

Many wonder if success like this can be sustained. Six years later, in 2011, I hosted a visiting superintendent from Washington state. He wanted to see a turn-around school (one that was previously failing and now succeeding), so I took him to Viers Mill. In every classroom, and we visited a lot of them, great teaching was happening and students were enthusiastically learning. The principal, Matt Devan, and his lead teacher, Susan Freiman, showed us something mind blowing. Two years earlier, in 2009, they decided that having 95 percent of their students succeeding in reading and math wasn't good enough. Why couldn't they shoot for 100 percent? In 2010, they did it. Even though more students than ever were living in poverty, were highly mobile, and were learning English, 100 percent of their fifth graders were reading and doing math on or above grade level.

Einstein said, "Once we accept our limits, we go beyond them."[11] If you believe the roadblocks you encounter are not going to limit you, it becomes possible to achieve incredible things.

Whether you're a teacher, an administrator, or a member of any team or office, it's an important leadership lesson—to succeed at levels higher than ever before, **ACCEPT NO LIMITS.**

Notes

1 Distributed by Universal Pictures, 2004.
2 Music by Hoagy Carmichael, lyrics by Stuart Gorrell, 1930, Hal Leonard Corporation.
3 Ray Charles, Atlantic, 1954.
4 Ray Charles, Atlantic, 1959.
5 See http://thinkexist.com/quotation/once_we_accept_our_limits-we_go_beyond_them/221878.
6 It qualified as a Title I school—a federal government designation meaning it served a large low-income community.
7 Bandura, Albert. 1986. *Social Foundations of Thought and Action: A Social Cognitive Theory.* Prentice-Hall. Englewood Cliffs, NJ.
8 Skinner, B. F. 1948. *Walden Two.* Hackett Publishing. Indianapolis, IN. Revised 1976 edition.
9 Freud, Sigmund. 1949. *The Ego and the Id.* Hogarth Press. London.
10 See http://www.goodreads.com/author/show/4467789.Mahatma_Gandhi.
11 See http://thinkexist.com/quotation/once_we_accept_our_limits-we_go_beyond_them/221878.
12 Dalai Lama. 2000. *The Dalai Lama's Book of Wisdom.* Thorsons. New York. See also http://www.bamboointhewind.org/teaching_dalaiquotes.html.

Reflection Activity 3

With the realization of one's own potential and self-confidence in one's ability, one can build a better world. According to my own experience, self-confidence is very important. That sort of confidence is not a blind one; it is an awareness of one's own potential. On that basis, human beings can transform themselves by increasing the good qualities and reducing the negative qualities.

His Holiness the Dalai Lama, from
The Dalai Lama's Book of Wisdom[12]

Just as Ray Charles did not accept limits others tried to place on his talent, you don't need to accept the artificial limits others try to place on you, your knowledge, or skills—or on the people you work with. As you complete the reflection activity below, resist the temptation to succumb to negativity or limiting thinking. Take to heart the teaching of the Dalai Lama. Be aware of your own potential, or as the psychologist Albert Bandura calls it, your self-efficacy.

Keep in mind the examples of kindergarten teacher Brenda Robins, who refused to allow MS to limit her ability to teach her students, and principal Jamie Virga and his staff who turned a school around. Think about the people in your life who accomplished their goals because they believed they should **Accept No Limits**.

Who do you know who has demonstrated **Leadership Lesson 3: Accept No Limits**? What did they do and say? Be as specific as possible. What did you learn from them that you want to apply to your own life and work?

_____

_____

_____

_____

_____

_____

_____

_____

_____

_____

_____

_____

_____

_____

_____

_____

Reflect further by doing the self-rating scales below. If this leadership lesson is one you have just started using, you are at the beginning phase. If you are using this leadership lesson regularly, you are now at the practicing phase. Like expert musicians we need to commit to practicing these lessons for our entire careers and lives. When you have mastered this leadership lesson and incorporated it naturally into your repertoire, you have reached the leading level.

Rate yourself using this scale. Mark a place on the line that represents _your_ current state on **Leadership Lesson 3: Accept No Limits**.

1	2	3	4	5
Beginning		Practicing		Leading

Rate your team, department, school, office, business, or organization using this scale. Mark a place on the line that represents *your group*'s current state on **Leadership Lesson 3: Accept No Limits**.

1	2	3	4	5

Beginning   Practicing   Leading

What commitment will you and the people with whom you work make to fulfill this leadership characteristic? How can you incorporate the leadership lesson of **Accepting No Limits** into your life and work? What concrete action steps will you take? What will be the sequence? What timeline will you follow?

Commitment:

_____

_____

_____

_____

_____

_____

Action Steps	Person(s) Responsible	Timeline

George Gershwin

LESSON 4:
Be Eclectic

George Gershwin
Credit: Photofest

GEORGE GERSHWIN—that talented, prolific composer and songwriter. Thinking about his memorable music and the sheer astounding output, before his untimely death from a brain tumor at the much too young age of 38, is just mind boggling. How could he possibly have written it all?

He wrote songs for musicals with his brother, Ira, like "Our Love Is Here to Stay"[1] and "I Got Rhythm,"[2] that have become standards in the American songbook, funny songs for the hilarious Marx Brothers' comedies, and longer, ground-breaking compositions for orchestras; he could do it all. Who can forget the piece whose beginning was inspired by the sound of French taxis—"An American in Paris"?[3] Or the one that starts with that long-sweeping clarinet glissando—"Rhapsody in Blue"?[4]

The Gershwin score of the opera *Porgy and Bess*[5] had unforgettable songs like "Summertime" and "I Got Plenty of Nothin'." To even consider writing an opera with a black cast, about people living in poverty in rural South Carolina, who sang in dialect to a mixture of classical European musical forms along with American jazz and folk music, was unheard of. People were shocked! It broke the rules of what opera was expected to be, just as "Rhapsody in Blue" broke the rules about what serious orchestral music was supposed to sound like because it put jazz on the concert stage. *Porgy and Bess* was not a financial success. It ran for only 124 performances and closed. Now, however, it is considered an American classic and performed all over the country and the world. When the Kennedy Center in Washington, D.C. put it on, it sold out so quickly that they had to simulcast it on the national mall and public television.

What lesson can we learn from George Gershwin, who wrote so successfully in an impressive variety of musical styles?

BE ECLECTIC

The Lesson Goes to School: How Educators Can Be Eclectic

Just as Gershwin wrote in so many styles successfully, we need to be able to teach in whatever manner it takes to help our students learn. One method just won't do it. Teachers know that students are complex human beings, with diverse patterns of strengths and needs. Classrooms are even more intricate, because they are individual complexity times the 25 or 30 students in a class. This multiplies the patterns into an intricate web of requirements that demand various approaches if a teacher is to have any chance of succeeding. Teaching is a challenging profession and there is truth in the old saying: the only people who think teaching is easy are people who have never taught.

Schools are even more complicated because they are complexity multiplied by several hundred or more diverse students. When you add the complexity of the strengths and needs of the staff and parents, you have a multi-faceted society as challenging to lead as any company or town. Schools are also different from one another; all of them are unique combinations of the unique individuals who comprise them.

While this may seem self-evident, it's surprising how often we think that there is *one* way, and not surprisingly it's always *our* way, the way we are used to, the right way to handle everything. It takes a certain amount of courage and open-mindedness to embrace the eclectic approach of George Gershwin—finding the best fit for each circumstance and each person.

Education professors and other people who train teachers often talk about an instructional strategy called differentiation: teaching each student in the specific way he or she needs. This sounds overwhelming to most people when first introduced to the idea. There is a way, however, to think about meeting so many needs that makes it possible and practical and connects to the importance of being eclectic like George Gershwin. Jon Saphier, Mary Ann Haley-Speca, and Robert Gower wrote a useful book about this strategy called *The Skillful Teacher*.[6] It summarizes the research of hundreds of studies about good teaching and organizes them in an accessible way. While no one can possibly absorb and then practice all the techniques they recommend, everyone can use the main idea of the book—an idea they call *matching*—learning to use as many new teaching strategies as possible to broaden our repertoires, and then matching the right strategy to the unique needs of each student and class. Saying we believe in this approach is very different from doing it successfully and doing it with a full heart.

Allie Ground always taught with her heart leading the way. During 19 years at Brown Station Elementary, she taught second, third, fourth, fifth, and sixth grade. No matter what their ages, she was loved by her students. They could feel her deep dedication. I knew she was a special teacher because I taught sixth grade down the hall, and her former students always talked about her with a combination of love and awe. Later on, she taught social studies to eighth graders at a nearby junior high, and she discovered that she had a special connection with the school's struggling students. They had a kind of gravitational attraction to her, often spending their lunch periods in her classroom, just to be with their favorite teacher a little longer.

When I became a high school principal a few years later, I had a vacant teaching position, and it was one of the hardest jobs to fill. Alternative education teachers work with at-risk students, those who have failed repeatedly and experienced years of disappointment. It's a group of students who usually have trouble with reading, writing, and math, and who also usually have a lot of behavior problems resulting from years of frustration. Who would want a job like that; a job that is almost guaranteed to lead to burn-out?

To my great surprise, Allie called me asking if she could have the job. She felt it was her mission, a sort of calling, to transform the lives of those who needed her the most. I didn't know if she could do it. After all, to work with bitter, depressed, and angry high school juniors and seniors is a far cry from teaching elementary school or even junior high, but my wife Joanie, with her usual good judgment, said, "Hire her. Allie can do anything!"

In her first few months on the job, Allie practiced her signature style of high-expectations teaching, with constant messages about her belief in her students' abilities accompanied by a take-no-prisoners form of discipline. There would be no bad behavior or not doing homework in her class. She would give a student a big hug, and while their faces were inches apart she would quietly, but firmly, say: "I love you. Now sit down and finish your homework." This approach was working pretty well, but it was a struggle to get kids to cooperate who hadn't been good students for a long time, if ever.

Allie noticed a 16-year-old boy becoming increasingly withdrawn. She made repeated attempts to talk to him, but each time she was rejected. With the perseverance I came to understand was an ineradicable part of her character, she finally got the message through to him that she could be trusted, and he was able to share with her the heartbreaking situation that his younger brother had cancer and was dying. With his permission, she started visiting the family's apartment. The family was so focused on taking care of the dying boy that they had stopped taking care of themselves and of everything else. No shopping, no cooking, no cleaning—nothing was being done. They were immobilized, sitting frozen in their pain and sorrow.

Allie began helping them with household chores. She showed up at school with a trunk load of plastic bags full of dirty laundry. A whole group of teachers and other staff volunteered to take it home and do the washing and ironing so that Allie could return everything clean to the family.

All the while, Allie's class watched her, amazed by what they saw. Even though she had taught for over 25 years, she was a new teacher to them, and new teachers have to prove themselves. This new teacher was demonstrating a commitment to a student's wellbeing that they had never witnessed before. They were won over. Allie's class of at-risk students saw a teacher who cared more about them than probably anyone else ever had. What a powerful lesson!

They started calling her by a new name. No longer was she "Mrs. Ground." Now she was "*Mama* Ground." They began doing more of their homework. They would arrive at her classroom door at six in the morning to do their work before school. At lunchtime, she would give them special, personal hall passes so they could go to the cafeteria to pick up their lunches and eat with her in her classroom while doing their assignments. Mama Ground ended her day by staying after school to tutor those who needed extra help.

I wish this story ended with a miraculous cure for the boy. Unfortunately, Allie's student's sick brother died. Everyone went to the funeral. There were tears and hugs and a period of the deepest sadness. But there was also something else.

Mama Ground's alternative education class had become a family. They had learned first-hand that caring for one another and the bond of grief could make their lives compassionate, fuller, and better.

In all the jobs she held, Allie practiced what some call *tough love*, firmness that communicates caring. People who say they are using *tough love* usually put the emphasis on the word *tough*. Allie put the emphasis on *love*. Her determined insistence, her consistency, her reliability, and her unwillingness to accept that her students should be treated as less than they were capable of being was all a manifestation of her love.

What makes a teacher do what Allie did for her student's family? At bottom, it's a sincere desire to help others beyond the duties of your job description. This story could just as easily have been in Chapter 1. Allie Ground, just like Sharon Jones and Denise Schaeffer, was the embodiment of the first leadership lesson—**Be Sincere**. In addition to her obvious sincerity, Allie possessed the motivation and skill to do whatever it took to meet her students' needs, whether they were in fourth grade, eighth grade, or high school; whether they had trouble reading, doing math, learning social studies, or controlling their feelings. She had the perseverance and ingenuity to **Be Eclectic**, drawing from her inner and outer resources to make good things happen for others.

Years later, I was giving a tour of our school to the newly appointed central office director of alternative programs. He wanted to know why we were getting such good results with our most challenging students. I told him the answer was a teacher named Allie Ground. We stopped outside Allie's classroom, just as a large young man in his twenties came down the hall. When he saw Allie, he threw his arms around her, hugging her with all his might, lifting her feet off the floor. "Mama," he beamed, "I've got a job!" The director nodded and said, "I see what you mean."

Although we might easily accept the idea that being eclectic is necessary for effective teaching, when it comes to leading a grade level, department, or school, it's strange that we often think of our leadership style as an immutable part of our personality. A formerly effective teacher who adapted teaching strategies to meet students' needs could become a supervisor with a "take-it-or-leave-it, that's who I am" attitude.

We certainly don't need to think about leadership in this rigid way. I have known some leaders who successfully modeled eclecticism. It worked beautifully for them and their schools. Equally important, it meant a lot to the people who worked with them.

Marty Barnett was an instructional specialist at Summit Hall Elementary, in Gaithersburg, in a part of town that was one of the poorest communities in the county. His job was to help the staff improve their students' academic performance. It was a huge challenge; many of the children came to Summit Hall with big gaps in their knowledge and skills. To motivate students, he set up tutoring programs and established partnerships with local businesses which provided backpacks and school supplies, and also incentives and awards to recognize their accomplishments. He spent all of his waking hours finding resources so that the students would have what they needed to succeed. The results of his efforts were impressive. Students' attendance improved, as did their report-card grades and test scores.

Later in his career, Marty became the principal of Cold Spring Elementary, in the suburb of Potomac, one of the wealthiest communities in the state and country. He committed himself with equal enthusiasm to helping these students achieve excellence. At Cold Spring, he didn't need to bring in outside resources. The school was set financially due to the high socio-economic level of the parents. He soon realized that he needed to make a different kind of contribution this time, to the school climate. He started by getting to know every student in a personal and inviting way. He learned their names, their interests, their strengths, and their areas of weakness. He found out who needed a little encouragement, an individual conversation, or some counseling.

Here, too, he achieved great results. Not only did the students continue to score in the top of the nation, but the students and parents felt that he had helped make the school a warmer, more nurturing and inviting place—a place where he and the staff personally knew and valued every child.

In both schools, Marty gave of himself with all of his energy. However, in the two different schools, he had to vary his way of operating. His basic belief in how to treat people remained solid. The types of activities he developed, the kinds of resources he found, and the personal actions he took had to be flexible. Marty was eclectic, and therefore he succeeded in both places; always making sure the children and schools were taken care of, no matter what he needed to do to make that happen.

BE ECLECTIC—a lesson all great leaders of their classrooms, schools, or other organizations take to heart, because they know one size never fits all. Eclectic leaders have the power to adapt their leadership styles to their people's strengths and needs, to help them become what they are capable of being. They understand further that, in their own lives, eclecticism enables them to grow, so they can fulfill their own potential and, in so doing, help others fulfill theirs.

Notes

1   "Our Love Is Here to Stay," music by George Gershwin, lyrics by Ira Gershwin, copyright 1938 by Gershwin Publishing Corporation, copyright renewal assigned to Chappell and Co.

2   "I Got Rhythm," music by George Gershwin, lyrics by Ira Gershwin, copyright 1930 by W. B. Music Corporation (renewed).

3   "An American in Paris," music by George Gershwin, copyright 1928 by W. B. Music Corporation (renewed).

4   "Rhapsody in Blue," music by George Gershwin, copyright 1924 by W.B. Music Corporation.

5   *Porgy and Bess*, music by George Gershwin, lyrics by Ira Gershwin, copyright 1935 (renewed 1962) by George Gershwin Music, Ira Gershwin Music, and Dubose and Dorothy Ward Memorial Fund, all rights administered by W.B. Music Corp.

6   Saphier, Jon, Haley-Speca, Mary Ann, and Gower, Robert. 2008. *The Skillful Teacher: Building Your Teaching Skills*. 6th edition. Research for Better Teaching. Acton, MA.

7   Powell, Colin. (n.d.). BrainyQuote.com. Retrieved July 23, 2012 from http://www.brainyquote.com/quotes/quotes/c/colinpowel393609.html.

Reflection Activity 4

Fit no stereotypes. Don't chase the latest management fads. The situation dictates which approach best accomplishes the team's mission.[7]

Colin Powell, American statesman

As a general, national security advisor, chairman of the Joint Chiefs of Staff and as secretary of state, Colin Powell modeled the power of eclecticism. He understood that there is never a one-size-fits-all solution, especially to a complex problem in the world of international diplomacy. The very eclectic George Gershwin wrote in many different styles to solve different sets of musical problems, whether creating a romantic ballad, show tune, opera, or concert piece.

This lesson, **Be Eclectic**, isn't easy to adopt. We have a natural tendency to do what we have done before; to replicate our actions because of what we learned from our previous experiences. This is why it's so important to seek intentionally to widen our repertoires and match the right actions to the people and situation. As you complete this reflection activity, remember Allie Ground's outreach to her student and his family and the ways Marty Barnett adapted to two schools with very different needs. Think about the people in your life who succeeded because they demonstrated that they could **Be Eclectic**.

In your life and work, who do you know who has demonstrated **Leadership Lesson 4: Be Eclectic**? What did they do and say? Be as specific as possible. What did you learn from them that you want to apply to your own life and work?

_____

_____

_____

_____

_____

_____

_____

_____

_____

_____

_____

_____

_____

_____

_____

_____

Reflect further by doing the self-rating scales below. If this leadership lesson is one you have just started using, you are at the beginning phase. If you are using this leadership lesson regularly, you are now at the practicing phase. Like expert musicians we need to commit to practicing these lessons for our entire careers and lives. When you have mastered this leadership lesson and incorporated it naturally into your repertoire, you have reached the leading level.

Rate yourself using this scale. Mark a place on the line that represents your current state on **Leadership Lesson 4: Be Eclectic**.

1	2	3	4	5

Beginning   Practicing   Leading

Rate your team, department, school, office, business, or organization using this scale. Mark a place on the line that represents *your group*'s current state on **Leadership Lesson 4: Be Eclectic**.

1	2	3	4	5

Beginning   Practicing   Leading

What commitment will you and the people with whom you work make to fulfill this leadership characteristic? How can you incorporate the **leadership lesson of being eclectic** into your life and work? What concrete action steps will you take? What will be the sequence? What timeline will you follow?

Commitment:

_____

_____

_____

_____

_____

_____

Action Steps	Person(s) Responsible	Timeline

Duke Ellington

LESSON 5:
Lead by Participating

Duke Ellington (1899–1974)
Credit: Private collection/Bridgeman Art Library

DUKE ELLINGTON—my personal all-time favorite legend. "Take the 'A' Train"[1] was his signature tune. Surprisingly, he didn't write it. His friend and frequent collaborator Billy Strayhorn wrote it. That intriguing detail provides a clue to what made Duke Ellington's leadership style extraordinary.

A young man growing up in Washington, D.C., Edward Kennedy Ellington liked to wear fashionable clothes and look sharp. As teenagers tend to do, his friends mocked him: "What do you think, you're a king, a prince or duke or something?" The nickname "Duke" stuck.

When Wynton Marsalis, Jazz at Lincoln Center's artistic director, teaches master classes, he evaluates the Duke Ellington Orchestra as the greatest band in the history of the Earth and Ellington as one of the most important composers of the past century.[2]

There is a powerful lesson we can learn from Duke Ellington about how to lead.

My friend Michael plays cello in the Dallas Symphony Orchestra. He once asked me, "What do you think most classical musicians think of symphony conductors?"

I thought for a while. "If you are selected for the position of conductor to lead a symphony orchestra, it must mean you are held in the highest regard for your musical knowledge and ability. I would guess the musicians are in awe of them."

"Wrong!" he quickly responded. He lifted his hand, the way a conductor holds a baton, and said, "We always say, 'How much music does he get out of that little stick anyway?'"

Take another look at Duke. On the following page you can see him when he was a little older.

What is he doing? What is the difference between him and the symphony conductors my friend was criticizing? Duke is conducting with only one hand; he's playing the piano with the other hand. While he leads his musicians, at the same time he participates with them in the music making.

He felt so strongly about this approach that he not only played the piano while conducting, he often composed with members of his band in mind. He listened closely to how they played, and learned their particular strengths and styles, and then wrote especially for them, taking advantage of what they could do as musicians and highlighting them as performers. It's no surprise that many of his band members spent decades with him, legendary musicians like Johnny Hodges, Cootie

Portrait of Duke Ellington and Sonny Greer, Aquarium, New York, November 1946
Credit: William P. Gottlieb, Gottlieb Collection assignment no. 455

Williams, Bubber Miley, "Tricky Sam" Nanton, Ben Webster, and Paul Gonsalves. Who wouldn't want to stay with a leader who listens so intensely and appreciates talent so deeply?

Musicians like Billy Strayhorn had the talent to compose; Duke welcomed that, playing their pieces or collaborating with them. Maybe he was generous. Maybe Duke was plain smart. He used the ideas and creativity of those he worked with and produced some of the best music of the century: "Take the 'A' Train," "Satin Doll,"[3] "Mood Indigo,"[4] "Sophisticated Lady,"[5] "Come Sunday,"[6] "It Don't Mean a Thing (If It Ain't Got That Swing)."[7] Can you imagine the respect Duke Ellington had from his band? Not only did he write but he wrote for them; not only did he play but he played with them. That is the leadership lesson we can learn from the great Duke Ellington:

LEAD BY PARTICIPATING

The Lesson Goes to School:
How Educators Can Lead by Participating

I have known less than a handful of principals who taught a class while also running their schools. Benjamin Banneker Middle School's Fred Lowenbach taught a study skills course for sixth graders. It's the kind of class that teachers are rarely keen to take on because it introduces kids to middle school and focuses on the basic skills you need to succeed— organizational skills, note taking—not a very exciting curriculum. Because it was a class that lasted for one marking period so that by the end of the year all the new middle-school students had taken it, Fred saw it as an opportunity to personally get to know all of his students and, as they say in the jazz world, to not "lose his chops" as a teacher. It amazed me that he was able to do this; I was a middle-school principal too and barely keeping my head above water. When he later became principal of a big, busy high school, his overly full schedule meant that he could no longer teach regularly. He confessed to me that it was one of the things he missed the most, so he asked the teachers if he could become a guest teacher in their classes.

Like the best hands-on administrators, he created other ways to get out of the office to be with his students and staff. I once saw a group of his African American male students who had started a club do a presentation about how they help each other with their schoolwork to keep their grades up. When I asked them to say hello to Mr. Lowenbach for me, every one of them not only knew their principal, but they told me that he knew them personally and enthusiastically supported the work of their group. Clearly, Fred had found other ways to **Lead by Participating**.

I've known other principals who modeled the concept of **Lead by Participating**. Kathy Brake was the long-serving principal of Washington Grove Elementary School, a small school in a high-poverty community. When the school put on a play, there was Kathy up on stage playing the role of some outrageous character, with her students and staff applauding a leader not afraid to have a little fun at her own expense. Eric Davis, the principal of Montgomery Village Middle School, sang to his students when they had Peace Days—days without teasing or fighting. Mike Durso, principal of Springbrook High School, had everyone laughing at a Homecoming Pep Rally by dressing up as a female cheerleader. These may seem like small symbolic acts, but they are important because they communicate the message of a leader who body and soul is all in, totally committed and fully participating with their staff and students.

Many principals **Lead by Participating** by doing the small things that demonstrate solidarity with their staff. Once as I was showing a Board of Education member around my school, as I bent down to pick something up for the third time, she said, "What is it with all of you principals? Every time one of you gives me a tour, you spend every other minute picking up trash off the floor."

That's what principals who participate do. They pick up trash when they walk down the hall, not expecting that it's solely the job of the custodial staff to keep the school clean. They handle some of the behavior referrals to the office themselves, instead of delegating all the discipline cases to an assistant principal. They stand outside and greet the buses and help the drivers if they have a problem with a student. They eat lunch standing up while doing cafeteria duty. They substitute for a teacher in an emergency. They attend staff-development training workshops with their teachers instead of just poking their head in the door. They facilitate decision making by consensus instead of asking someone else to work out a problem. They personally mentor a student. They are involved as much as anyone— probably more.

The idea of **Lead by Participating** has its roots in the work of one of America's most important leadership theorists. James MacGregor Burns was a presidential biographer, Pulitzer Prize and National Book Award winner and professor of government at Williams College. Burns distinguished between two concepts. One style, transactional leadership, is based on a give-and-take relationship, in which the supervisor and the employee trade interests such as salary, working conditions, perquisites, or promotional opportunities for improved productivity.

Transforming (later called transformational) leadership changes the lives of people and organizations by enhancing morale, motivation, and performance—the characteristics we want in every employee. This form of leadership even has the potential to change followers into leaders. Imagine the power of an organization in which all employees feel they should take the initiative and responsibility of leaders. There would be no stopping a school or a company in which everyone acted so energetically. The fundamental question is: if we want to be transformational leaders, how does **Lead by Participating** help us get there?

Here is how Burns describes when transformational leadership is taking place. "Transformational leadership occurs when one or more persons engage with others in such a way that leaders and followers raise one another to higher levels of motivation and morality."[8] The phrase that could easily be missed is "engage with others." He doesn't say "direct others," or "delegate to others." He says "engage with others"—the idea that what great leaders do is work along with others. It's Ellington playing along with his band, or principal Fred Lowenbach teaching along with his faculty, or principal Kathy Brake acting along with her students. They're all engaging with others. They are **Leading by Participating**.

There is more to the idea of transformational leadership than the requirement of engaging with others, but it is the essential piece, without which the other components don't work. Burns says that, while engaging with others, transforming leaders behave in four main ways. They mentor or coach their employees, providing empathy and support. They stimulate and encourage creativity. They motivate, challenge, and communicate optimism about accomplishing future goals. (Remember the importance of **Leadership Lesson 2: Be Optimistic**.) They are role models for ethical behavior (which we will explore further in Chapter 7, **Be Strong by Being Principled**). A leader who demonstrates all of these characteristics will earn the respect and trust of everyone.

We shouldn't think of the transforming idea of engaging with others in these ways as solely the responsibility of the principal or the head of any organization. It can raise the bar for leadership at any level.

Becky Sanderoff was the chairperson of Colonel Zadok Magruder High School's math department. When she arrived she had been an elementary- and middle-school teacher and had even taught math courses at the local community college, but she had never taught high-school students. The high-school math teachers naturally viewed her appointment with suspicion. She may have had an advanced degree in math education, but she had never worked at their level. How could she understand their world?

The head of a high-school math department can choose to teach whatever courses she wants. In most cases, the department chair picks the most advanced classes—calculus, advanced statistics. It's a lot of fun and very satisfying teaching the highest-achieving and most motivated students in a school. The math teachers were shocked when Becky assigned herself the most difficult and frustrating course in the school—double-period algebra—the course for the weakest math students who hadn't been able to pass algebra in middle school because they lacked so many basic skills.

The head of a department usually has the decision-making power to choose a nice office, with windows to provide light, air, and a view, and to choose a nice classroom, spacious and convenient to her office and the faculty rest room. In the same high school where Becky headed the math department, Grant Goldstein was the chair of the English department. The school was overcrowded; although built for 1,900 students it had more than 2,300 students enrolled, far over capacity. This meant that some teachers would have to float—to share classrooms and move from room to room. In many schools, the newest teachers, those who can least afford to bear the burden, are not assigned their own classrooms and are given schedules requiring them to move throughout the day, making it even more difficult for them to establish structure and get their lessons off to a good start. Grant and Becky planned the schedules with their teachers to ensure fairness. They put their own materials on rolling carts and, along with their teachers, floated for part of the day to show their overworked colleagues that they were willing to endure all of the same inconveniences.

Whereas department heads are leaders of teachers, teachers are leaders of their students and can also set a powerful example when they **Lead by Participating**. We know that students are always watching their teachers (just as they watch their parents) and what they see teachers *do* means more than what they *say*, which is, of course, true for all leaders. Imagine a third-grade teacher showing a video on photosynthesis and how plants grow or a high-school civics teacher showing a video on the checks and balances of our three branches of government. Chances are the teachers have already seen these videos many times before. They have probably seen them so many times that they can recite some of the lines by heart.

For teachers, the most important commodity is time. There is never enough time to do everything a good teacher has to do: grading papers, preparing lessons, responding to administrators, or returning parent phone calls and emails. There just isn't enough time during a school day to get it all done. This becomes a moment of temptation. While the video is playing, the teacher can grade a few tests, or answer an email from a concerned parent.

The students don't know that their teacher has seen the video a hundred times. They don't care that the teacher already knows all the information in the video. All they see is a teacher doing something else while they are supposed to be focused on the screen. What do they conclude? The video must not be very important. Their teacher isn't watching it. The result will be perfectly predictable. They won't pay attention. They will get distracted. They may even start misbehaving.

Imagine if the teacher introduces the video by telling the students how important the information is that they are about to see. The teacher stops the video occasionally to ask a question or emphasize a key point. Now the students are focused and learning. Now the teacher is engaged with the students. Now the teacher is **Leading by Participating**.

Fred Lowenbach, Becky Sanderoff, and the others knew that one of the most important keys to successful leadership is to engage and participate with others, in order to contribute to the day-to-day operation of the school. There is a lot of unglamorous work a leader does behind closed doors to keep a school or department or classroom running smoothly, and most people never see, nor even know, those parts of the job exist. When a principal teaches a class or substitutes for a teacher who has an emergency, or a head of department teaches the most exhausting course or suffers the same daily hardships as the members of the department, or a teacher does an activity along with her students, everyone sees them **LEAD BY PARTICIPATING**. The power of example is far greater than anything you can achieve behind closed doors.

Notes

1   Words and music by Billy Strayhorn, copyright 1941. Dimensional Music of 1091 (ASCAP) and Billy Strayhorn Songs, Inc. (ASCAP). Rights for Dimensional Music of 1091 and Billy Strayhorn Songs, Inc. administered by Cherry Lane Music Publishing Company, Inc.

2   De Vise, D. 2007. From Marsalis, a Master Class in "That Swing" and the Ellington Exhortation. *Washington Post*. April 19. Montgomery Extra. P. 9.

3   Words and music by Johnny Mercer, Duke Ellington, and Billy Strayhorn, copyright 1953, 1958 Music Corp., Famous Music Corporation, and Tempo Music (copyright renewed).

4   Words and music by Duke Ellington, Irving Mills, and Albany Bigard, copyright 1931 (renewed 1959) and assigned to Emi Mills Music Inc., Famous Music Corporation, and Indigo Mood Music in the U.S.A.

5   Words and music by Duke Ellington, Irving Mills, and Mitchell Parish, copyright 1933, Sony/ATV Music Publishing LLC and Emi Mills Music Inc. in the U.S.A.

6   From *Black, Brown, and Beige* by Duke Ellington, copyright 1946 (renewed). By G. Schimer Inc. (ASCAP).

7   From *Sophisticated Ladies*. Music by Duke Ellington, words by Irving Mills, copyright 1932 (renewed 1960). Emi Mills Music Inc., Famous Music Corporation in the U.S.A.

8   Burns, J. M. (1978). *Leadership*. Harper and Row. New York.

9   Bruce Springsteen quoted in Remnick, D. 2012. We Are Alive. *New Yorker*. July 30. P. 42.

Reflection Activity 5

The three most important ways to lead people are: . . .
by example . . . by example . . . by example.

Albert Schweitzer, medical missionary
and philosopher

Many of Duke Ellington's musicians played in his band for their entire careers because he led by example, modeling through his participation—composing for them and playing with them. James MacGregor Burns would have called him both a transactional leader (responsible for salaries and working conditions) and a transformational leader (engaging with the musicians and raising their motivation).

Similarly, there are still members of the original E Street Band playing on tour with Bruce Springsteen, who writes the songs as well as plays and sings, as he leads his band by example. Springsteen once said, "The band is a little community up there."[9]

Like Ellington and Springsteen who each created a community of musicians on stage, and like the principals and teacher leaders in this chapter who created communities in their schools and departments, we can create our own communities, too, which can only be accomplished through authentically engaging with, counting on, and respecting our colleagues' ideas, styles, and talents.

Consider the differences between Ellington and the symphony conductor, and remember the principals, department heads, or teachers you have known who **Lead by Participating** with their staff and students, and those you have known who do not lead this way. We all want to work with leaders who are truly with us.

In your life and work, who do you know who has demonstrated **Leadership Lesson 5: Lead by Participating**? What did they do and say? Be as specific as possible. What did you learn from them that you want to apply to your own life and work?

_____

_____

_____

_____

_____

_____

_____

_____

_____

_____

_____

_____

_____

_____

_____

_____

Reflect further by doing the self-rating scales below. If this leadership lesson is one you have just started using, you are at the beginning phase. If you are using this leadership lesson regularly, you are now at the practicing phase. Like expert musicians we need to commit to practicing these lessons for our entire careers and lives. When you have mastered this leadership lesson and incorporated it naturally into your repertoire, you have reached the leading level.

Rate yourself using this scale. Mark a place on the line that represents _your_ current state on **Leadership Lesson 5: Lead by Participating**.

1	2	3	4	5
Beginning		Practicing		Leading

Rate your team, department, school, office, business, or organization using this scale. Mark a place on the line that represents *your group*'s current state on **Leadership Lesson 5: Lead by Participating**.

1	2	3	4	5

Beginning   Practicing   Leading

What commitment will you and the people with whom you work make to fulfill this leadership characteristic? How can you incorporate the **leadership lesson of leading by participating** into your life and work?

What concrete action steps will you take? What will be the sequence? What timeline will you follow?

Commitment:

_____

_____

_____

_____

_____

_____

Action Steps	Person(s) Responsible	Timeline

Leonard Bernstein

LESSON 6:
Lead with Imagination

Leonard Bernstein
Credit: Photofest

IT WAS 1957. On Broadway, Shakespeare's classic *Romeo and Juliet* was transplanted to New York City. The warring Montagues and Capulets became two rival street gangs, the Jets and the Sharks. The composer was Leonard Bernstein. His amazing, groundbreaking idea was the now classic *West Side Story*.[1] This set the stage for more unorthodox subjects

(*RENT*,[2] *Sweeney Todd*,[3] *The Producers*,[4] *The Book of Mormon*[5]). Back in the late 1950s and early 1960s a show like *West Side Story* was visionary and revolutionary, which points us to the lesson we can learn from Leonard Bernstein:

LEAD WITH IMAGINATION

The Lesson Goes to School: How Educators Can Lead with Imagination

Although leading with imagination is sometimes a little scary, it's not really as risky as you might think. Take, for example, John Ceschini, the principal of a small, quiet school in Prince George's County, Maryland—Rockledge Elementary School. It was a school no one had ever heard of. It was literally off the radar, hardly noticed even by the superintendent or his staff.

When John was starting out and getting to know his teachers, his students, and their parents, he noticed that there was a core group of people who loved art, music, and theater. John talked to his staff and the parents in the PTA and then took a leap of faith. He declared the school "Rockledge Elementary—the School for the Arts."

It's very important to understand that no one had given John permission to make this proclamation; he just did it, as the Nike commercial recommends. And because he did it, some remarkable things started happening. They started applying for grants from arts organizations and, to their surprise, received some of them. John joined the Kennedy Center's Principals' Forum for the Arts. That opened the door to training for Rockledge's teachers so they could learn how to infuse music, art, theater, and dance into their teaching and enrich their students' learning experiences, creating what we would now call an integrated or interdisciplinary curriculum. The Kennedy Center even began to send performers to put on free assemblies, so the students would be introduced to classical music, opera, jazz, ballet, and theater.

Before long, people did take notice. The school system embraced the idea, even heralding it as a model program. As the old saying goes: success has a thousand fathers, but failure is an orphan. The idea of an elementary school for the arts was clearly a winner, so everyone got on board and even took a little credit. Achievement went up. The school won awards. John became the *Washington Post* principal of the year for his county.

West Side Story wasn't Bernstein's only leap of imagination. He was the first one to hold Young People's Concerts[6] on television to bring the love of classical music to children. He wrote his own *Mass*.[7] He conducted orchestras all over the world. He collaborated on a musical version of Voltaire's classic story *Candide*.[8] He never stopped creating as he stretched his mind and his talents.

That's also an important part of this lesson: **Lead with Imagination**. It inspires us to keep being creative, to keep imagining how we can be better and how we can make our schools, our work, and our lives more enriched and fulfilling.

The act of imagining an improved future is what leadership and management theorists call having a vision. Peter Drucker, probably the most famous management writer and consultant of the twentieth century, said it simply and best: "Leadership is vision."[9] It's certainly the starting point. As a new principal, John Ceschini imagined a school with a theme that excited everyone, made them want to be there and feel motivated to do their best work.

But no leader can do it alone. A vision the leader holds, but isn't shared by others, goes nowhere. Peter Senge, the author of one of the most influential books on change, maintains that having a shared vision is essential. He says: "People learn to nourish a sense of commitment in a group or organization by developing shared images of the future they seek to create."[10] John Ceschini could see that the arts provided a way to make his image of the future real; they were a means of moving the teachers and parents to action—and moving the school toward achieving the shared vision of a creative, wonderful place for children.

When good ideas take root they produce such positive energy that other ideas are generated. After the arts theme was well established, John and his staff did something imaginative again; they started a sister school partnership with a school in England. Every year a student and family, along with a staff member, went to England for two weeks, and English visitors spent the same time in Maryland. When a school is led by a leader with imagination, everyone begins to dream of new possibilities. Even a forgotten little school can break new ground, can improve, can become proud, and can be excited about what it is achieving.

Best-selling author Daniel Pink promotes the importance of leading with imagination, too. He argues that having lived through the agricultural age, industrial age, and information age, we now live in the conceptual age where creativity and innovation make the difference in being successful in today's environment.[11] While many people have read his book with the goal of learning how businesses can gain a competitive edge, his idea that the future will be determined by people who are inventive and empathetic, who see the big picture and who can make meaning, applies equally well to classrooms, schools, and all other groups, teams, and organizations.

Every school or office has someone who is an early adopter[12]—the person who is not only willing to experiment with the newest technology, but is chomping at the bit to get started. Douglas Root was an eighth-grade social studies teacher who couldn't wait to bring computer applications into his classroom. He was recording his students' grades in an electronic grade book long before it became common practice, and just as we saw that John Ceschini's idea of a school for the arts led to further creativity, Doug had the same habit of thinking beyond current boundaries.

Many students living in poverty went to Gaithersburg Middle School. We saw this in Chapter 1 when we learned the leadership lesson **Be Sincere**, about how Sharon Jones, the principal of the nearby elementary school, went with the school counselor door to door in the soon-to-be demolished Lee Street apartments, showing the families how sincerely she wanted to help them give their children stability by remaining in their school as they dealt with the unsettling change of moving.

In their frustration about finding a way to raise their students' achievement levels, the middle school's leadership team of administrators and teachers found themselves discussing interesting questions: did their students think school was important for their futures? What did their students imagine they would do for a living when they were adults? Since they didn't know the answers, they decided to do an unscientific survey and each ask ten students what they wanted to be when they grew up. When they got together again the following week, they reported their findings. Many of the students wanted to be singers, performers, or athletes, but few saw themselves as having a career that required study after high school.

The middle-school teachers and administrators wanted their students to improve their achievement and then do well in high school so that they could eventually go to college. Now that they knew so many students didn't see themselves in professions requiring a college degree, they asked themselves if their students recognized the connection between going to college and having greater career options. Could the students even picture themselves on a college campus someday? Had any of them ever visited a university? It was time for another unscientific survey.

The following week they reported back that almost none of their students had ever been on a college campus, except for the few who had been to a University of Maryland Terrapins basketball game. Maybe, they thought, if they took their students to college for a day, they could plant the seed of an idea—that college was in their future. They would walk on a beautiful campus, tour the impressive facilities, and see students carrying their books and socializing on their way to class. It would be such an attractive picture that students would aspire to be a part of it.

Now that they had a goal of every middle-school student going to college for a day, the next question was how to prepare for this unusual field trip. They started calling local colleges and, at first, received a cold reception. Whoever heard of taking middle-school students to college? Weren't they too young? Was this really a good use of the college's resources? The staff persevered and eventually did find a few colleges willing to try this early college visit experiment. At the same time, the counselors and parents wrote to colleges across the country requesting posters which they then stapled to bulletin boards all over the school in every hallway, classroom, and office. Everywhere the middle-school students walked, they saw pictures of smiling college students on attractive campuses.

Doug took the preparation of his students to an even higher level. He worked with a team of teachers to create lessons connecting the skills they usually taught as part of their curriculums to the idea of going to college. The social studies teacher did a geography lesson on where the colleges are located. For the first time, students who had heard about the Fighting Irish football team of Notre Dame learned that the university is in Indiana. The math teacher asked the students to solve an authentic word problem: if tuition is now $15,000 and increases at a rate of 5 percent per year, as it has for the past ten years, then how much will tuition cost when you are a college freshman? The English teacher explained to her students that when they applied to college they would need to write an essay to convince the admissions committee that they should be accepted. This became a very realistic persuasive writing assignment—and an early first draft of their future admissions essay. Doug, our technology early adopter, took his classes to the computer lab so that they could take a virtual tour of the campus and investigate the courses they would be required to take for their major and the extracurricular activities they could participate in to have an enriched college experience.

By the time the eighth graders went on their college field trip they were psyched, they were prepped, and they were ready with questions they wanted answers to. They came home energized and with so much information for their parents (and for their younger brothers and sisters too). Everyone quickly appreciated that the idea of a day at college had been a life-changing experience. The following year, the sixth and seventh graders as well visited different colleges with similar success. Because of the leadership team's creative thinking and willingness to innovate, the middle school had a college preparatory theme. When they asked students, in future years, what they wanted to do for careers someday, the kids had plenty of ideas, and they even knew the colleges where they wanted to apply and the grades they needed to earn so that they would be accepted and on the path to reach their goals. With such clear intent, even the transition to high school went more smoothly.

To think with creativity, to innovate, to lead with vision— that is the power of the lesson we learn from Leonard Bernstein's *West Side Story*, from John Ceschini's school for the arts, and from Doug Root taking his middle-school students to college. We can all **LEAD WITH IMAGINATION.**

Notes

1 *West Side Story* (1957). Music by Leonard Bernstein and Stephen Sondheim, book by Arthur Laurents, copyright 1957 Amberson Holding LLC and Stephen Sondheim. Copyright renewed 2007 by Amberson Holding LLC and Stephen Sondheim, Leonard Bernstein Music Publishing Company LLC, publisher Boosey and Hawkes Inc., sole agent.

2 *Rent* (1996). Words and music by Jonathan Larson, copyright 1996 Finster and Lucy Music Ltd. All rights controlled and administered by Universal Music Corp.

3 *Sweeney Todd* (1979). Music and lyrics by Stephen Sondheim, copyright 1979 Rilting Music, Inc. All rights administered by W. B. Music Corp.

4 *The Producers* (2000). Music and lyrics by Mel Brooks, copyright 2000 Mel Brooks Music (BMI).

5 *The Book of Mormon* (2011). Words and music by Trey Parker, Robert Lopez, and Matt Stone, copyright 2011 Only for Now, Inc. and Furry Carlos Music Publishing, Inc. All rights on behalf of itself and Only for Now, Inc. Administered by Warner-Tamerland Publishing Corp.

6 Young People's Concerts. Retrieved August 12, 2012 from: http://www.leonardbernstein.com/ypc.htm.

7 *MASS: A Theater Piece for Singers, Players, and Dancers* (1971). Music by Leonard Bernstein, text by Bernstein and additional text and lyrics by Stephen Schwartz. Premiered September 8, 1971 as part of the opening of the John F. Kennedy Center for the Performing Arts in Washington, D.C. Retrieved August 12, 2012 from: http://www.leonardbernstein.com/mass.htm.

8 *Candide* (1956). Music by Leonard Bernstein, book by Lillian Hellman (after Voltaire), lyrics by Richard Wilbur, John LaTouche, Dorothy

Parker, Lillian Hellman, and Leonard Bernstein. Retrieved August 12, 2012 from: http://www.leonardbernstein.com/candide.htm.

9   In Senge, Peter et al. 1999. *The Dance of Change: A Fifth Discipline Resource.* Currency Doubleday. New York. P. 16.

10 Ibid. P. 32.

11 Pink, Daniel. 2005. *A Whole New Mind: Why Right-Brainers Will Rule the Future.* Riverhead Books. New York.

12 The term "early adopters" originated in Rogers, Everett M. 1962. *Diffusion of Innovations.* Free Press. Glencoe, NY.

13 Caro, R. A. 1981. *The Path to Power.* Vantage Books. New York.

Reflection Activity 6

He didn't know whether what he was going to try would work, the new President said: "I tell you frankly that it is a new and untrod path." But he was going to try. "I tell you with equal frankness that an unprecedented condition calls for the trial of new means." And if these means didn't work, he said, he would be the first to admit it. And then he would try something else.[13]

Robert Caro, biographer, on Franklin Delano Roosevelt's response to the Great Depression

The most respected leaders are not afraid to try new ways of achieving a vision. What President Roosevelt did for the country, what principal John Ceschini and his staff and parents did for their elementary school, and what teacher Doug Root and his team did for their middle-school students required leaps of imagination, or what change researcher Peter Senge called "shared images of the future."

No one except Leonard Bernstein and his talented collaborators thought a musical about gangs in New York was a promising idea, and no one had previously thought it was a good idea to transform an overlooked school into a school for the arts or to expand students' personal career goals by taking them to college. For any of these accomplishments to have been attained, or for any dreams we hope will become reality, it takes people who **Lead with Imagination**.

Who do you know who has demonstrated **Leadership Lesson 6: Lead with Imagination**? What did they do and say? Be as specific as possible. What did you learn from them that you want to apply to your own life and work?

_____

_____

_____

_____

_____

_____

_____

_____

_____

_____

_____

_____

_____

_____

_____

Reflect further by doing the self-rating scales below. If this leadership lesson is one you have just started using, you are at the beginning phase. If you are using this leadership lesson regularly, you are now at the practicing phase. Like expert musicians we need to commit to practicing these lessons for our entire careers and lives. When you have mastered this leadership lesson and incorporated it naturally into your repertoire, you have reached the leading level.

Rate yourself using this scale. Mark a place on the line that represents _your_ current state on **Leadership Lesson 6: Lead with Imagination**.

1	2	3	4	5
Beginning		Practicing		Leading

Rate your team, department, school, office, business, or organization using this scale. Mark a place on the line that represents *your group*'s current state on **Leadership Lesson 6: Lead with Imagination.**

1	2	3	4	5

Beginning   Practicing   Leading

What commitment will you and the people with whom you work make to fulfill this leadership characteristic? In other words, how can you incorporate the leadership lesson of **Lead with Imagination** into your life and work? What concrete action steps will you take? What will be the sequence? What timeline will you follow?

Commitment:

_____

_____

_____

_____

_____

_____

Action Steps	Person(s) Responsible	Timeline

Marian Anderson

LESSON 7:

Be Strong by Being Principled

Marian Anderson, Lincoln Memorial Concert
Credit: National Film Registry/Photofest © National Film Registry

IN THE 1930s, Marian Anderson was America's best and most celebrated contralto. Her debut with the New York Philharmonic was a huge success, and in 1928 she sang in Carnegie Hall. She then toured Europe to universal acclaim and gave 70 stellar performances all over America.

Still, by 1939, she had never sung in a concert hall in our nation's capital, only in D.C.'s schools and churches. Her manager, Sol Hurok, decided it was time for her to sing where the best musical performers sang when they were in Washington, in D.A.R. Constitution Hall.

The Daughters of the American Revolution refused adamantly to let a "singer of color" perform on their stage. Public outrage followed, and first lady Eleanor Roosevelt resigned her membership from the D.A.R. At Mrs. Roosevelt's suggestion, the Secretary of the Interior, Harold Ickes, invited Ms. Anderson to sing from the Lincoln Memorial in a free concert for whoever would like to attend. On Easter Sunday, April 9, 1939, 75,000 people came to hear Marian Anderson. It was the largest concert ever held on the Mall, with millions more Americans listening at home on their radios.

Standing in front of the giant statue of Abraham Lincoln, she began the concert with "America," singing the stirring words "My country 'tis of thee, sweet land of liberty, of thee I sing." As University of Pennsylvania curator Nancy M. Shawcross put it, "Although a difficult and painful incident for Ms. Anderson, it remains a touchstone for all those who have struggled to gain racial equality in the United States."[1] The leadership lesson we can learn from Marian Anderson is:

BE STRONG BY BEING PRINCIPLED

The Lesson Goes to School:
How Educators Can Be Strong by Being Principled

Be Strong by Being Principled doesn't mean being tough like a bully or using your power or authority to force your viewpoint. It's not meant as a "my way or the highway" idea. Instead, it means that there is positive power in standing our ground the way Ms. Anderson did and holding firm to our values. It commands attention, attracts allies, and often wins the day. In their hearts, people want to do the right thing. This is especially true in schools and in other helping professions where people are motivated by doing good for others, which is the reason they entered these professions in the first place.

Thomas Sergiovanni, the highly respected author of articles and books about educational leadership, teaches that the best leaders "know the difference between real toughness and merely looking tough or acting tough. Real toughness is always principle-value based . . . They are outraged when they see these values ignored or violated."[2] How does this idea of strength through sticking to your principles play out in real life?

One of my most memorable supervisors, and one I grew to greatly admire, was someone who knew how to lead by being principled. Dr. Janet Bergman was a tough-minded lady who could intimidate you with a questioning glance or, worse yet, a frown. Upon meeting her for the first time, it became immediately clear that she knew more about teaching than we did, and more than any professor we had studied with in college. She had read the research, she had observed in hundreds of classrooms, she had evaluated all those teachers; in short, she knew her stuff. When I first went to work for her, she made me nervous, and I found out pretty much everybody felt that way, too. If ever there was a values-driven leader, it was Dr. Bergman.

For a few years, she ran a summer program for young children who couldn't read. If she visited a classroom and saw bad teaching, she was hard to restrain. She felt that the kids were being cheated. If she saw a teacher mainly lecturing and not giving the students a chance to practice their reading, she would be outraged and ask, "Would a basketball coach *talk* about basket-ball for the entire practice? NO! He *shows* the team how to play and then they *practice, practice, practice*! And that's what children need to do to learn how to read. They don't need *lectures*. They need *modeling, coaching*, and *practice!*"[3] The next time we visited that classroom, you can bet the teacher was helping the students practice their reading.

There is an old saying in management literature: a good administrator is a balance of task orientation and human orientation.[4] In Dr. Bergman's case, she was often more direct than diplomatic. But if you watched how she arrived at decisions, you always saw that they were student-centered, because her values were fixed and unchanging over time. And there was no time to waste. Kids deserved the best education and she wouldn't rest until they were receiving it, regardless of whether her decisions were popular. As a result, she might not have always been well liked for her hard-driving style, but there was no doubt that she was well respected for her rock-solid values. As a result, thousands of children benefited from her unrelenting commitment. That is what it means to: **Be Strong by Being Principled.**

Coaches can also inspire us to go beyond everyone's expectations through principled leadership. One of my favorite coaches (of many great coaches I've known) is Paul Foringer who was the varsity boys' basketball coach at Gaithersburg High School. Even though he inherited a losing franchise when he took the job, he insisted that his players be true student-athletes. He required them to go to class on time, respect their teachers, behave appropriately, and be academically eligible, maintaining at least a 2.0 grade point average (a G.P.A. which equals a grade of C on an A–F scale).

I once saw him bench his tallest and best player for repeatedly being late to school. The boy's mother called the coach because she couldn't get her son to come home before midnight, so the coach started calling their home at 9:00 every evening to make sure he was there. The boy wasn't benched for a few minutes of the game or for the first quarter; he had to dress in a collared shirt and tie and sit on the bench to support his team mates for the next three games. After his team lost the third game without him, possibly jeopardizing the team's regional ranking in the *Washington Post*, he started coming home on time.

Then Coach Foringer did something really amazing. One day at practice he called his players together and asked them, "Do you want to be a starter? Do you want to hear your name announced over the microphone at the beginning of the game? Do you want to hear the cheerleaders cheering, and the band playing, and the lights flashing and the crowd roaring when you come running off the bench slapping fives with your team mates?" "YEAH!" his players yelled back at their coach. "Then you need a 2.5," he said.

He had done something that no one had ever heard of. He had raised the grade point average from 2.0 (C) to 2.5 (C+/B–) for starting players. You had to have a higher G.P.A. than the county school system required if you wanted to start for Coach Foringer and Gaithersburg High.

Oh, did the coach take some grief for that! Even though he put tutoring and mentoring programs in place to help his students reach the higher bar, it didn't stop the players complaining to each other and to the assistant coaches. Their parents complained and filed appeals with the principal and school system. The fans complained and booed if their favorite players were missing from the starting line-up. Threats were made and the coaches started walking to their cars in groups after games. But to his credit, the coach stood his ground. And to his principal's credit, when parents demanded that he fire the coach, the principal, Fred Evans, supported his coach. That took courage, because even though Fred was an experienced middle-school principal, this conflict happened during his first year as Gaithersburg High School's principal, and the last thing a first-year high-school principal wants is a sports controversy.

What did the complainers say? They argued that you wouldn't win games if you raised the standards. In other words, you couldn't be competitive on the court if you required higher achievement in the classroom. Even worse, they argued, because other schools weren't doing it, you were putting your team at a competitive disadvantage. Didn't the coach know that not only was the school's reputation at stake and school spirit was going to decline, but there were potential scholarships at stake? Didn't he know what he was risking?

All of those voices were silenced in 1998 when the Gaithersburg High School Trojans made it to the state play-offs, facing the traditionally favored basketball powerhouse, Oxon Hill High School of Prince George's County, in the most exciting high-school game anyone had ever seen. Busloads of fans from both communities packed Cole Field House at the University of Maryland. No one could believe it, there were one, two overtimes played. Then, in the third overtime, Gaithersburg kicked in a buzzer beater to stay alive leading to a fourth overtime and then, unbelievably, a fifth overtime was played. We screamed so loud we were all hoarse the next day.

When the last jump shot swished through the basket and Gaithersburg had won the state championship, never was there so much glory and celebration in the history of the school. Never again was there a complaint that you had to accept a low level of academic achievement to have a high level of athletic competitiveness.

Real toughness, maintains Sergiovanni, means sticking to your principles, whether you are an administrator like Janet Bergman, whose most important value was insuring every student learned to read, or a coach like Paul Foringer, who believed winning athletes could be successful students too, if you held your ground, or a singer like Marian Anderson who held onto her values and kept her faith in her country's promise of equal treatment for all, and years later returned triumphantly to sing on the stage at Constitution Hall. Results are often hard-earned. That is the reward and the joy when you remember to **BE STRONG BY BEING PRINCIPLED.**

Notes

1   Shawcross, Nancy M., curator. 2011. *Marion Anderson: A Life in Song*. Penn Library/exhibitions. Annenberg Rare Book and Manuscript Library, University of Pennsylvania, at: http://www.library.upenn. edu/exhibits/rbm/anderson/lincoln.html.

2   Sergiovanni, Thomas J. 2001. *The Principalship: A Reflective Practice Perspective*. Allyn and Bacon. Boston, MA. P. 155.

3   Bergman, J. 1992. SAIL: A Way to Success and Independence for Low Achieving Readers. *Reading Teacher* 45(8).

4   Bass, Bernard M. and Bass, Ruth. 2008. *The Bass Handbook of Leadership: Theory, Research, and Managerial Applications*. 4th edition. Free Press. New York.

5   Stewart, John. 2012. Bruce Springsteen's State of the Union. *Rolling Stone* 1153(March): 42.

Reflection Activity 7

I have faith that through pressing on and through paying attention and listening and being vigilant and voicing your concerns and insisting that the right thing be done, you can move your world inches closer to where you want it to be for your children. You have to have faith in that. You have to have a clear eye, but you still have to have an open heart and mind. Because you have to have spirit, you have to have the soul.

Bruce Springsteen, musician, composer[5]

The great Marian Anderson, administrator Janet Bergman, and coach Paul Foringer had the faith to hold onto their overriding principles and the strength, as Bruce Springsteen says, to press on. Due to Dr. Bergman's perseverance, hundreds of teachers learned how to be better reading teachers and thousands of young children learned to read. Because of Coach Foringer's uncompromising efforts, hundreds of students became true student-athletes and proudly graduated high school, and a community learned a valuable lesson about the importance of setting high standards. Because Marian Anderson was a woman of integrity and strength, the door to equality for everyone opened a little wider. To paraphrase the Boss: they moved their world inches closer to where they wanted it to be for children and for future generations.

Who have you known who stayed the course to do what they thought was right, even at the risk of loss of popularity or support? How did they live **Leadership Lesson 7: Be Strong by Being Principled**? Taking a values-based stand, even on a matter some may consider small, takes courage. What did you learn from them that you admire and want to emulate?

_____

_____

_____

_____

_____

_____

_____

_____

_____

_____

_____

_____

_____

_____

_____

Reflect further by doing the self-rating scales below. If this leadership lesson is one you have just started using, you are at the beginning phase. If you are using this leadership lesson regularly, you are now at the practicing phase. Like expert musicians we need to commit to practicing these lessons for our entire careers and lives. When you have mastered this leadership lesson and incorporated it naturally into your repertoire, you have reached the leading level.

Rate yourself using this scale. Mark a place on the line that represents _your_ current state on **Leadership Lesson 7: Be Strong by Being Principled**.

1	2	3	4	5
Beginning		Practicing		Leading

Rate your team, department, school, office, business, or organization using this scale. Mark a place on the line that represents *your group*'s current state on **Leadership Lesson 7: Be Strong by Being Principled**.

1	2	3	4	5

Beginning   Practicing   Leading

What commitment will you and the people with whom you work make to fulfill this leadership characteristic? In other words, how can you incorporate the **leadership lesson of being strong by being principled** into your life and work? What concrete action steps will you take? What will be the sequence? What timeline will you follow?

Commitment:

_____

_____

_____

_____

_____

_____

Action Steps	Person(s) Responsible	Timeline

Frank Sinatra

LESSON 8:
Train to Grow

Portrait of Frank Sinatra and Axel Stordahl, Liederkrantz Hall, New York, 1947
Credit: William P. Gottlieb, Gottlieb Collection assignment no. 455

FRANK SINATRA—what a phenomenon he was! When he first went out on his own, the young girls, the "bobbysoxers," screamed, and women of all ages swooned.

The leadership lesson exemplified by Frank Sinatra happened before he became so famous. He was working with the Tommy Dorsey orchestra as a band singer and still developing his distinctive style. Frank realized that if he was going to compete for attention on stage with the great musicians in the band, and compete for fans' attention with all the other boy singers on the dance band circuit, then he would not only have to *hit* the notes, he would have to be able to *hold* the notes longer and clearer than anyone else. How do you teach yourself to do that? Frank found an answer in an unusual place—the local swimming pool.

If you take a deep breath and dive into the water, then keep holding your breath as you swim, you eventually increase your lung capacity. Each time Frank went swimming, he practiced holding his breath until, after a while, he could hold his breath a long time. He found he could hold notes a long time, too. When he was up on the stage, he could now compete for the spotlight with any instrument. Those long notes also made him stand out from all the other boy band singers of the day. This was the key to the style that got him the attention and billing he needed to eventually go out on his own as a solo act. The rest is history. He became a sensation.[1]

The essential leadership lesson we can learn from Frank Sinatra is:

TRAIN TO GROW

The Lesson Goes to School:
How Educators Can Train to Grow

There are three key points to remember from the Frank Sinatra swimming story.

First, all excellent leaders need to understand the importance of training. As leaders of classrooms, schools, companies, government agencies, or non-profits, or simply as leaders of our own lives, we always have to think about the training others need and, probably even more important, that we, ourselves, need. Stephen Covey, in his best-seller, *The 7 Habits of Highly Effective People*,[2] called this habit *sharpen the saw*, reminding us of the importance of renewing ourselves in every way: physically, spiritually, mentally, and socially/emotionally. He says this is so important that it "surrounds the other habits . . . because it . . . makes all the others possible."[3]

Beyond our personal development, it's just as important that we keep learning so that we model the belief in continual growth. It's essential that we keep providing opportunities for learning so that our students or employees feel supported. With all of the demands placed on schools, businesses, and other organizations today—especially with scarce resources and increased competition and accountability—it's easy to feel overwhelmed. Relevant, high-quality training, offered in a way that people can accept and view as helpful, is one of the best ways of reducing anxiety, while, at the same time, increasing the capacity to work more effectively and efficiently.

The second key point is to remember that training doesn't have to appear to be directly related to the goal. We shouldn't think of training in a narrow sense. For Sinatra, the swimming increased his capacity to hold notes. He didn't take singing lessons or just keep practicing on his own to learn how to hold notes longer. He did something unusual to prepare himself to accomplish his goal.

The third key point is to acknowledge that training can't be a one-shot deal, sometimes referred to as "drive-by training," a phrase which captures accurately the idea of training offered too fast and too disconnected from people's daily work and lives. Research has clearly shown that we shouldn't think of training in the traditional "come to a workshop and then go back to work" scenario. We've all been to workshops that made no difference to our professional or personal lives. Rather, we ought to embrace the idea of professional development that is ongoing and authentically connected to people's real needs.

Imagine you want to learn to play tennis. It takes a while to teach someone to play, especially to play well, and if we really want you to learn, we won't send you to sit in a workshop in a hotel conference center to hear a lecture and watch a demonstration. Instead, a pro would work with you on the court to teach you to serve or adjust your backhand. Just as the pro hits you the ball, watches you swing and then models better form so your swing improves, that is the way to provide meaningful training— coaching people at their actual work site (or at least in simulated real-life scenarios), so they can gradually upgrade their skills. A motivational speaker or a seminar isn't necessarily a bad way to begin, but it's no replacement for on-site (or what some call job-embedded) coaching.

The same principle of **Train to Grow** applies to any job or specific area in which we want to improve and become proficient. For example, we want our children's math skills to improve and achievement scores to go up so they can compete with students from other countries. Then we, as a nation, can successfully compete technologically and economically. The typical response is to keep training teachers on how to implement the math curriculum. But the training might need to be about other aspects of effective teaching such as questioning and checking for understanding, using assessments or data analysis tools, or about relationship building with students—especially hard-to-reach kids.

For some teachers, the training might need to be delivered in an unconventional way, perhaps with someone modeling better approaches in their own classrooms. The traditional approach of reviewing the math curriculum in a workshop and requiring teachers to learn to teach it in a mechanical, scripted way might not produce the type of teacher who can inspire students to approach math with real enthusiasm.

My friend Sandy Dugoff taught me how to teach writing to sixth graders in a way that combined all three keys to effective training. Sandy was a language arts specialist. She had been a terrific reading teacher and then became an equally skilled trainer of teachers. One day, our principal introduced the four members of our sixth-grade team of teachers to Dr. Sandra Dugoff. He asked us to work with her to find ways to improve our students' writing. He wasn't wrong about their skills. We were pretty frustrated with their short and often poorly written sentences, paragraphs that didn't hold together and papers that varied widely in quality from pretty good to downright awful. None of us wanted to sit through hours of in-service training on how to teach writing. Sandy could sense our defensiveness, and she made us an offer we couldn't refuse. She said, "Give me any group of students you've got, and I'll teach them to write. But there's only one catch. Whatever group you give me, you have to participate along with your students so that you'll learn the process as children experience it. Only then will you feel comfortable teaching it later on."

I took her up on her offer, and I must admit I agreed because I had the lowest functioning reading group—the kids who came to sixth grade reading on the third- and fourth-grade level. I thought she couldn't do it and that this would prove that it wasn't my poor teaching that was the problem, but that the students I had were very hard to teach. Boy, was I wrong!

Sandy taught my writing class every day for a couple of weeks. I sat in a student desk and did every assignment along with my kids. Before long I saw a remarkable difference in their writing—and mine. She had a system that was blame free. It allowed, even encouraged, kids to get their thoughts on paper without worrying about being perfect. Don't know how to spell a word? Take your best guess and get the thought on paper and look it up later, but don't stop the flow of ideas at that moment. Not sure where to start a new paragraph? Just keep writing, even if you go a whole page or two without a new paragraph. We'll find the places where the ideas shift later and indent when we revise. Can't think straight after a while because you've been staring at your essay for so long? Soon you'll get a chance to work with a partner who will look at it with fresh eyes.

I'm not suggesting that the way Sandy approached writing instruction is the only way, but what's important (and what was a brand new experience to me) was that it brought the training into my classroom so I could experience it first-hand. It also took away all my excuses for not doing something different. It opened me up to new possibilities, and when she left, I had to admit she was a better writing teacher than I was, and I wanted someday to be able to be half as good. I not only adopted her methods, but we became lifelong friends, because I wanted to keep learning from someone with as much to offer as she had.

My experience learning how to teach writing also illustrates an important consideration in training, what Stanford University social and developmental psychology professor Carol Dwek calls the concept of *mindset* or "the view you adopt for yourself."[4] Here is how she describes the two views:

> Believing your qualities are carved in stone—the *fixed mindset*
> —creates an urgency to prove yourself over and over.[5]
>
> This *growth mindset* is based on the belief that your basic qualities are things you can cultivate through your efforts. Although people may differ in every which way—in their initial talents and aptitudes, interests, or temperaments— everyone can change and grow through application and experience.[6]

As I look back on this training experience, it is now clear to me that I began with a fixed mindset. Like a lot of people who have tried to do a good job, I felt I had done my best. So whose fault was it that the students weren't learning to write? Not mine. I was working hard and I had even tried several different approaches. Mostly what I had done was to put out a lot of effort, but I was getting nowhere. So when Sandy made her offer, I felt threatened. If she succeeded with my students, then the problem was with me, not with them. So I offered her the hardest-to-teach kids, feeling pretty sure of myself that she wouldn't be able to do it. I could feel satisfied that I was a good teacher, but the odds were stacked against me.

Something happened that I hadn't expected. Because she insisted that I participate along with the kids, Sandy was preparing me to have a growth mindset. She was telling my students that they could write—and write well. They just needed to learn some more effective strategies. As I was sitting alongside them, I was hearing the same message. Because I was learning the same strategies, I was finding that the writing came easier. In fact, I don't think I would have written this book if not for Sandy's insistence on my experiencing good writing instruction first-hand.

Sandy had combined several of the approaches of **Train to Grow**: high-quality training, delivered in a non-traditional way, and done in my own work site over time. These methods opened me up to the possibility that I could become a better writing teacher. In Carol Dwek's terms, I went from a fixed to a growth mindset because of this powerful training experience.

Some people are self-starters and can't wait to learn. They have what Carol Dwek calls "true self-confidence": "the courage to be open—to welcome change and new ideas regardless of their source."[7] They are a teacher's or a trainer's dream come true. Here are three of the lifelong learners I've known.

Bonnie Leister is a principal who embodies the idea of **Train to Grow**. She is always reading research about how to improve teaching and learning, and discussing with her staff how they can teach better so their students will learn better. Her school is constantly improving and it's no surprise that her students are always excelling. She reads widely, she attends conferences, she teaches university courses; she takes advantage of every opportunity to grow professionally. Whenever I see her I can count on her asking me if I'd seen a certain journal article or tried a new technique. Then she asks me if I've read or tried anything new and interesting lately, because if I have, she wants to know about it. Even after many years of being a principal, there is an undiminished feeling of excitement about Bonnie's work, and it comes from embracing and living the principle **Train to Grow**.

Sometimes you're lucky enough to meet someone who inspires you with their love of lifelong learning. At the time of this writing, Paul Williams is in his eighties. He had a long and successful career in Washington, as General Deputy Assistant Secretary for Fair Housing and Equal Opportunity, where he was responsible for the daily operation of the nation's Fair Housing Programs. He earned the Distinguished Service Award (which is the highest government services award) and is listed in *Who's Who* in America. After he was retired for many years, Paul made a decision to not only keep living an active life, but to find new ways to learn and grow and to contribute to the wellbeing of others.

He began conducting seminars for business and educational groups, schools, and senior centers in memory techniques, mental literacy, and reading, learning, and thinking techniques. Being an avid runner and athlete, he continued his ritual of running at least three miles early every morning and going to the gym, but decided to broaden his athletic interests by taking golf lessons, learning to play in his seventies.

As a member of the Rossmoor Kiwanis Club of Leisure World, a retirement community in Silver Spring, Maryland, Paul would visit the high school where I was principal to serve as an advisor to the high-school students in the Key Club, a service club doing good works for the community. The students loved him and viewed him as their mentor. Remember Allie Ground, the teacher of at-risk students in Chapter 4, **Be Eclectic,** who reached out to the family of her student? Before long, Allie had recruited Paul to teach her students Mind Mapping, a graphic organizing technique that helps students learn complex material. Paul was so successful teaching some of the hardest-to-reach students that Allie also asked him to help her with SAT-prep students using the technique to improve their SAT scores. Both the at-risk students' grades and the SAT-prep students' scores began going up and Paul became the guest teacher in demand, eventually teaching his strategies to many other teachers so they could start using them in their classrooms.

To this day, Paul Williams is still growing. He maintains that one of the keys to keeping your brain functioning at its peak as you grow older is committing yourself to learn new and challenging material, for example, to read, but to read out of your usual comfort zone so that you are continually making new neural connections. Now in his eighties, Paul continues to study, make presentations, and conduct seminars. Recently he organized a conference for students at a charter middle school in Washington, D.C. to expose them to scientists and other thinkers, in order to encourage them to think about planning to go to college and enter a scientific or technical field. Paul Williams continues to **Train to Grow** and I'm convinced he always will.

Peggy Bastien was a fourth-grade teacher at Rosemont Elementary, the first school where I served as principal. She had been teaching for over 25 years, in the same room! But contrary to the typical picture in many people's minds of a teacher who stays in one place for so many years, she wasn't a bit stale. The number of parent requests for Ms. Bastien to teach their children was overwhelming. She had taught their older daughters and sons, and now they wanted her to teach their younger ones. Why? They definitely knew what they would be getting: a high-quality, traditional education. What I learned by observing her was that, while her teaching style embodied many traditional values (respect, responsibility, perseverance), she was also constantly changing—trying new techniques that she had read about or learned in workshops; anything that might help her students improve.

Peggy knew that every group of children is different. When she began teaching math each new school year, she realized it couldn't be delivered exactly the same way as she had taught the year before. Every night she gave her students a hand-made worksheet to do for homework, not a worksheet she copied from a workbook, but one she created herself. Most of the page was filled with problems on that day's lesson. Two-thirds down the page she drew a line, and under that line were a few problems from earlier in the week or the week before. Under that section she drew another line, and below that line were the types of problems they had covered the previous month or last grading period. In other words, as the class moved forward, they also constantly reviewed recent concepts and older material.

I asked her how she had thought of this idea and she told me that she had read about students' retention of material and had seen the problem of kids forgetting first-hand, so she had developed this technique for helping them remember concepts and skills that they had previously covered. It was no surprise at all that year after year her students achieved the highest scores on standardized math tests. Was it more work for her to make a brand new homework sheet every night? Undoubtedly. But she took an idea she had learned and applied it even though it required more effort—and the benefits to her students were incalculable.

In Chapter 4's discussion of the fourth leadership lesson, **Be Eclectic**, we learned how eclecticism enables us, as leaders, to better serve others, and also helps us fulfill our own potential by expanding our repertoires and matching the right strategies and actions to what people need or situations require. If **Be Eclectic** is the *what*—what we need to become in order to be multi-faceted leaders and problem solvers—then **Train to Grow** is the *how*—how we learn to stay open and widen our field of vision to become multidimensional people who are capable of accomplishing much more than we had ever dreamed.

Notes

1 Lahr, J. 1997. Sinatra's Song. *New Yorker*. November 3, P. 76.
2 Covey, Stephen R. 1989. *The 7 Habits of Highly Effective People*. Simon and Schuster. New York.
3 Ibid. P. 287.
4 Dwek, Carol S. 2006. *Mindset: The New Psychology of Success*. Ballantine Books. New York. P. 6.
5 Ibid. P. 6.
6 Ibid. P. 7.
7 Ibid. P. 127.
8 Kennedy, John F., speech prepared for delivery in Dallas on the day of his assassination, November 22, 1963. See http://www.quotations page.com/quote/3225.html.
9 Dwek, *Mindset*. P. 127.
10 Kennedy, John F. 1962. Address at Rice University on the Nation's Space Effort. *Historical Resources*. September 12, John F. Kennedy Presidential Library and Museum. See http://www.jfklibrary.org/Historical+ Resources/Archives/Reference+Desk/Speeches/JFK/003POF03Space Effort09121962.htm. Retrieved August 16, 2010.
11 Kennedy, John. F. 1956. *Profiles in Courage*. Harper and Brothers. New York.

Reflection Activity 8

> Leadership and learning are indispensable to each other.[8]
>
> John F. Kennedy

Psychologist Carol Dwek would say that, as a leader, President Kennedy was a "possessor of true self-confidence" because he had "the courage to be open—to welcome change and new ideas regardless of their source."[9] Think of his challenge to us, as a country, to put a man on the moon, not only to win the space race, but because of the new knowledge that would be gained for science and education.[10] Kennedy's own Pulitzer Prize-winning book, *Profiles in Courage*,[11] celebrated public figures who put their principles first, much like we saw Marian Anderson do in Chapter 7's leadership lesson: **Be Strong by Being Principled**. In addition to being courageous, Kennedy clearly saw the essential bond between learning and leadership.

In this chapter's leadership lesson, **Train to Grow**, we saw how Frank Sinatra learned to hold notes through an unusual training method and how the reading specialist Sandy Dugoff, by bringing the training right into my classroom, not only taught sixth graders to improve their writing, but helped me become a better writing teacher, too. We also learned how Paul Williams continues to develop and contribute long after retirement and how great principals like Bonnie Leister and great teachers like Peggy Bastien always stay open, their constant search for new ideas making them ever better.

There are unlimited ways to **Train to Grow**. People who become the best at what they do, whether they are presidents, singers, principals, or teachers, always stay open and never stop learning. They apply what they learn to their work and their lives, which benefits them and the people they lead.

Who do you know who has demonstrated **Leadership Lesson 8: Train to Grow**? How did they demonstrate that they were not only open to new learning, but actively sought to enhance their knowledge and skills? What did they learn that enabled them to accomplish new tasks or overcome tough challenges? Be as specific as possible. What did you learn from them that you want to apply to your own life and work?

_____

_____

_____

_____

_____

_____

_____

_____

_____

_____

_____

_____

_____

_____

Reflect further by doing the self-rating scales below. If this leadership lesson is one you have just started using, you are at the beginning phase. If you are using this leadership lesson regularly, you are now at the practicing phase. Like expert musicians we need to commit to practicing these lessons for our entire careers and lives. When you have mastered this leadership lesson and incorporated it naturally into your repertoire, you have reached the leading level.

Rate yourself using this scale. Mark a place on the line that represents *your* current state on **Leadership Lesson 8: Train to Grow**.

1	2	3	4	5

Beginning   Practicing   Leading

Rate your team, department, school, office, business, or organization using this scale. Mark a place on the line that represents *your group*'s current state on **Leadership Lesson 8: Train to Grow**.

1	2	3	4	5

Beginning   Practicing   Leading

What commitment will you and the people with whom you work make to fulfill this leadership characteristic? How can you incorporate the leadership lesson of **Train to Grow** into your life and work? What concrete action steps will you take? What will be the sequence? What timeline will you follow?

Commitment:

_____

_____

_____

_____

_____

Action Steps	Person(s) Responsible	Timeline

Bob Dylan

LESSON 9:
Put the Message Across

March on Washington, close-up view of vocalist Bob Dylan, August 28, 1963

Credit: Rowland Scherman, National Archives and Records Administration, U.S. Information Agency. Unrestricted use

WHILE DRIVING TO A SCHOOL to consult with the principal, I was listening to an audio recording of Bob Dylan's autobiography.[1] He was talking about his early days in the 1960s, when he was singing and playing folk music in coffee houses in Greenwich Village. He said: "What really set me apart in these days was my repertoire . . . There were a lot of better singers and better musicians around these places, but there wasn't anybody close in nature to what I was doing. Folk songs were the way I explored the universe, they were pictures and the pictures were worth more than anything I could say. I knew the inner substance of the thing. I could easily connect the pieces."[2]

Then he added a thought which made me pull the car over to copy it down: "Most of the other performers tried to put themselves across rather than the song, but I didn't care about doing that. With me, it was about putting the song across."[3]

This is the leadership lesson we can learn from Bob Dylan. It's not about putting ourselves across. It's about putting our song, whatever it may be, across. In the situations in which we work and live, the lesson to remember is:

PUT THE MESSAGE ACROSS

The Lesson Goes to School:
How Educators Can Put the Message Across

With any kind of leadership, it's not about us, it's about the message.

Jim Collins, in his best-selling business book *Good to Great*,[4] calls this being a "Level 5 Leader." Level 5 leaders are personally humble, but very ambitious for their organizations. They don't see it as being about them, but about the success of their business or organization. Collins and his research team found that while the high-profile leaders written about in *Forbes* or *Fortune* magazines often received a lot of notoriety and increased profits for a while, their companies didn't sustain the success, especially after the charismatic leader was gone. Collins even thinks too much charisma can be a disadvantage.

Ms. Rafiya Senghor was a counselor beginning a new mentoring program for African American and Hispanic boys at an elementary school in a high-poverty area. Her principal, Lisa Thomas, invited me to see it in action. We stood in the cafeteria to observe the first session of the year. Ms. Senghor had everything organized, with donuts and juice laid out on a table for the students and their mentors, and some getting-to-know-each-other activities prepared to start everyone off on a friendly note. In her opening comments, Ms. Senghor set just the right tone: inviting yet businesslike. Participating was going to be fun, and at the same time the well-planned activities were going to be accomplished. During the introductions, when one little first-grade boy mumbled his name, she smiled and said, "Don't think you're going to come here and eat my breakfast and talk like that." The boy laughed and said his name out loud.

She had recruited nine men and matched each of them with one or two boys. As the men and boys were interviewing each other using a guide sheet she had provided, it was obvious how much they were enjoying the time together. While we looked on, I said to her, "What a beautiful program. I love how you structured it." Without hesitation, she replied, "It's a team effort; it's not just me. The teachers chose the students. The principal asked our business partners for donations for refreshments, and other staff recruited the mentors." Then she excused herself and walked back to monitor the activity. Rafiya Senghor is a Jim Collins, humble, Level 5 leader and also a Bob Dylan-style communicator who is all about putting the message across.

Collins also uses the metaphor of "the window and the mirror" to explain what great leaders do. When their organization is succeeding, they look out the window at their employees and give credit to everyone. When things aren't going well, they look in the mirror and see themselves, and take responsibility. That's counselor Rafiya Senghor who, when I complimented her for organizing an outstanding program, gave the credit to the whole team. That's also Lisa Thomas, the principal who invited me to see the new mentoring program her staff had set up, without in any way suggesting that she had been responsible, even though she had hired them (what Collins calls getting the right people on the bus), shown them the need for such a program, and encouraged their efforts.

Here is another more public example of a leader not being self-focused and never losing sight of the message.

I have seen many teachers and principals win awards for excellence or leadership. I was in Memphis conducting leadership training when the school system celebrated the candidates for principal of the year. After a slide show of the finalists in action the winner was announced, a distinguished gentleman with an ideal name for an educator who has earned everyone's affection— Dr. Love. He came forward and stood on the stage before his 600 colleagues. He said what the best principals and best leaders in all fields always say: "I'm so lucky to work with such a dedicated staff. We have talented and motivated students. We are also blessed to have caring and committed parents. We have a very supportive community. It's a team effort. We all collaborate. I feel lucky to be part of all of this."

Sometimes **Put the Message Across** has nothing to do with being given credit and everything to do with humbly giving to others. Here is the story of an inspiring teacher who did just that.

My wife, Joanie, was helping chaperone a school field trip with our son Ben's fourth-grade class and a fifth-grade class. On the long ride home with overtired students and exhausted adults, veteran fifth-grade teacher, Mrs. Phyllis Larsen, knew what to do to pass the time—she started a sing-a-long to the catchy military marching song, "Sound Off," making up her own words: "We went on a trip today. Saw the sights and we're on our way. Sound Off, 1–2. Sound Off, 3–4. Sound Off, 1–2–3–4, 1–2, 3–4."

Ms. Larsen noticed that some of the more energetic boys had started kicking the seats, probably for the sheer joy of watching the girls in front of them bounce up and down. A few of the seat cushions had come loose before she could stop them, so using this as inspiration, she now sang: "Sorry about the seats on the bus. You can blame it all on us." The kids sang this improvised verse with real enthusiasm. Oh, such fun, to think they were singing about themselves and their own bus trip (and their own slightly naughty behavior).

In the evening, as the bus slowly pulled into the school parking lot, the parents waiting to pick up their children left their cars and stood outside to greet them as they got off the bus. But they were surprised by what they saw. One red-faced boy, tears streaming from his eyes, came running down the steps, clutching the pillow he had brought from home. As Mrs. Larsen walked away, my wife watched in dismay as our son threw his pillow at her back.

His foot hit the curb and he took off, through the crowd of parents and across the parking lot and up the street, with mom chasing after him in the car, desperately urging him to get in. "Ben! Ben! What happened?"

Eventually she caught up to him. She looked her distressed child in the eyes: "Tell me, what's wrong?" And now sobbing, he said, "When Mrs. Larsen sang that song about the seats—she was looking right at me!! It's all my fault."

As Joanie finally convinced Ben to get in the car, she heard someone comment, "No child of mine would ever act so disrespectfully."

That night we waited for the inevitable call from the principal informing us that our son would be suspended from school for throwing an object at a teacher. We knew he would have to take his medicine and we would need to help him learn the right lesson from this experience. The phone rang. That wasn't the call we received.

To our surprise, we heard, "Hello, this is Ms. Larsen." Before she could say another word, my wife said, "Oh Ms. Larsen, we are so sorry. We feel just terrible. We talked with Ben and he definitely understands that what he did was wrong. He's working on a letter of apology to you right now. And he realizes he will need to accept any consequences the school gives him."

"Mrs. Steinberg, that's not why I'm calling," Ms. Larsen told the surprised mother. "I'm calling to apologize to Ben."

"Why would you be the one apologizing?" Joanie asked.

"Ben isn't in my class, but I know he is a good kid, and something must have set off such unusual behavior." The teacher continued, "I realize that it was the song I made up that disturbed him so, and I would never want to do anything that made a child feel so upset."

Ms. Larsen was a teacher much more interested in the message that a child received than in herself. She is the kind of teacher who, if you are lucky, passes through your child's life, recognizes his sensitivity, and molds it gently so it can become a positive trait in adulthood.

It would be easy to imagine a different scenario in which the teacher felt her safety or her dignity or her authority would be jeopardized if she permitted a child to get away with throwing something at her. What would the other students think? Would they ever take her seriously again? Classroom behavior would get out of control. This is not the way a Level 5 leader thinks. When things go badly, Jim Collins says, a great leader looks in the mirror, just as Ms. Larsen did, and takes responsibility.

Like the lyrics of a Bob Dylan song, the message is what's important. For leaders of a class, a school, a business, or any organization, the lesson here is to clearly communicate the message: when everybody contributes and works together, when everyone takes their egos out and puts their efforts in, then we succeed. Even when they are the ones being personally honored or individually tested, great leaders take every opportunity to **PUT THE MESSAGE ACROSS**.

Notes

1   Dylan, Bob. 2004. *Chronicles*, Volume 1. Simon and Schuster. New York.
2   Ibid. P. 17–18.
3   Ibid. P. 18.
4   Collins, Jim. 2001. *Good to Great*. HarperCollins. New York.
5   Albom, Mitch. 1997. *Tuesdays with Morrie*. Doubleday. New York. P. 43.

Reflection Activity 9

So many people walk around with a meaningless life. They seem half-asleep, even when they're busy doing things they think are important. This is because they're chasing the wrong things. The way you get meaning into your life is to devote yourself to loving others, devote yourself to your community around you, and devote yourself to creating something that gives you purpose and meaning.[5]

Morrie Schwartz, sociology professor,
Brandeis University

Mitch Albom's former professor, Morrie, inspired us with his message of finding meaning in our lives through loving others. As a teacher, Phyllis Larsen believed that a child's feelings were much more important than her own authority. Counselor Rafiya Senghor and principal Lisa Thomas knew that creating a mentoring program to change their young students' lives was what counted—not who received the credit. And Memphis principal Dr. Love gave an acceptance speech that was entirely about his deep feelings for his school and community—and not at all about himself. Like Bob Dylan in his songs, what was important to each of them was that they **Put the Message Across**, and their messages were about service to others.

Jim Collins would identify them all as Level 5 leaders because they were personally humble while completely devoted to creating something personally meaningful. When your words and actions communicate this message, then your leadership is much more likely to produce not only the results you need to achieve, but meaning and inspiration for yourself and for everyone working with you.

Who do you know who has demonstrated **Leadership Lesson 9: Put the Message Across**? What did they do and say? Be as specific as possible. What did you learn from them that you want to apply to your own life and work?

_____

_____

_____

_____

_____

_____

_____

_____

_____

_____

_____

_____

_____

_____

Reflect further by doing the self-rating scales below. If this leadership lesson is one you have just started using, you are at the beginning phase. If you are using this leadership lesson regularly, you are now at the practicing phase. Like expert musicians we need to commit to practicing these lessons for our entire careers and lives. When you have mastered this leadership lesson and incorporated it naturally into your repertoire, you have reached the leading level.

Rate yourself using this scale. Mark a place on the line that represents *your* current state on **Leadership Lesson 9: Put the Message Across**.

1	2	3	4	5

Beginning	Practicing	Leading

Rate your team, department, school, office, business, or organization using this scale. Mark a place on the line that represents *your group*'s current state on **Leadership Lesson 9: Put the Message Across**.

1	2	3	4	5

Beginning	Practicing	Leading

What commitment will you and the people with whom you work make to fulfill this leadership characteristic? How can you incorporate the leadership lesson of **Put the Message Across** into your life and work? What concrete action steps will you take? What will be the sequence? What timeline will you follow?

Commitment:

_____

_____

_____

_____

_____

_____

Action Steps	Person(s) Responsible	Timeline

Elvis Presley

LESSON 10:
Be Daring and High Energy

Elvis Presley
Credit: Photofest

"EXUBERANCE IS BEAUTY,"[1] said the poet William Blake, and if anyone exemplifies the combination of talent plus enthusiasm, it's The King— Elvis Presley. When he first appeared on national television on the Ed Sullivan Show, the censors wouldn't allow him to be shown from the waist down. Too sexy for America, they thought. The fans, mainly teenagers at first, knew they liked what they were hearing and seeing and they went wild. That combination of rebelliousness, excitement, and a mixture of great American musical traditions—a little bit of blues and soul and country and rock—all synthesized by an undeniably handsome, sexy, and yet appealingly nice young man. A little bit of danger along with the boy next door. When he started singing, swaying, and shaking, no one had seen audiences screaming in ecstasy like that since the swooning bobbysoxers made Frank Sinatra their idol.

What leadership lesson can we learn from Elvis? We want to follow leaders who possess the ability to:

BE DARING AND HIGH ENERGY

The Lesson Goes to School:
How Educators Can Be Daring and High Energy

There have been many movies about inspiring music teachers and for good reason. Just like a coach who takes a losing team and makes it a winner through a combination of skill, will-power, and perseverance (remember basketball coach Paul Foringer in Chapter 3's lesson, **Accept No Limits**), extraordinary music teachers can take a dissonant, dreadful-sounding band or chorus and transform it into a unified miracle of harmony. Maybe the biggest challenge of all is to accomplish this feat with an elementary school chorus.

Mark Amberg was that kind of teacher, but what made his accomplishment even sweeter is that he did it at an elementary school specially designed to accommodate students with physical disabilities. The chorus was open to everyone. Mark took all children who showed an interest in music or who said they wanted to sing—regardless of their ability—never turning anyone away.

Many music teachers hold auditions. It's natural to want to select the students with the most talent, or at least with the most potential. When a band or chorus performs, every person in the audience becomes a judge of talent. When the teacher takes the chorus or band to competition, then the stakes are even higher because actual judges with musical expertise rate their performance.

Yet Mark Amberg said yes to every student who wanted a chance to sing, and saying yes produced several results.

First, his chorus was twice or three times larger than anyone else's—and big musical groups are much harder to bring to a higher standard of musicianship than smaller ones. It's the same as the difficulty a teacher of a large class has raising the achievement of all her students or the challenge a leader faces bringing a large team or department or school to function at the highest level.

Second, larger music groups take much more energy and stamina by the teacher. There are simply more children to direct, to coach, or at a more basic level, to learn their parts, get on key, and stay in synch.

Third, because this was a school built to welcome students with physical disabilities (extra-large hallways, accessible seating, adaptive technology), many students who expressed interest in chorus needed assistance, and Mark had to figure out how to include them. Luckily, some kids had the help of para-educators who accompanied them and Mark collaborated with these assistants to make sure that the students could participate independently like all the other kids, with just as much individualized help as they needed. Sometimes he had to meet with the special education teachers, counselors, and parents to find a solution, but he always found one.

On concert days, the school's cafeteria was converted into an auditorium and it would always be packed with students, staff, parents, brothers and sisters, grandparents, and other relatives. But the concerts I remember most were the cluster concerts, in which all of the elementary-school, middle-school, and high-school choruses would take turns singing and the whole town would turn out to hear them. They were all good and it was a night of celebration. However, something special happened when Mark Amberg's chorus performed. There was always anticipation because we had to take an intermission so that Mark's chorus could get ready. So many students with disabilities participated that it took at least 20 minutes just to have the elevator next to the stage lift all of the kids in wheelchairs so they could get into position. Then there was the matter of there being so many students. Where the typical chorus had 20 or 30 students who could fit neatly on the stage and risers, Mark's chorus of 80 to 100 filled the entire expanse of the high-school stage from curtain to curtain.

When they sang, it was a phenomenon to behold. Not only did their sound fill the cavernous auditorium, but the joy on their faces moved everyone. So many students—many of them with disabilities—and all of them proud to be representing their school and singing their hearts out with every ounce of their being. Mark was working hard to keep everyone focused and on the beat, and he conducted with an energy that matched the kids' enthusiasm. Needless to say, they always brought the house down, and everyone went home inspired, having witnessed the magic and power of **Being Daring and High Energy**.

Eric Davis was a well-regarded principal of an elementary school who was promoted to run a middle school that the community thought was out of control. Parents heard stories about students misbehaving, teachers who were disheartened, and achievement that was declining as discipline problems were increasing.

Eric took the measure of his new school and concluded it was a place that no longer believed in itself. He decided to do something daring. He declared that there would be "Peace Days"—days in which no student would be sent to the office for serious misbehavior. At first, few believed him. After all, how could there be peaceful and productive days in a school that was largely perceived as chaotic? Eric understood that he had to back up his challenge with high energy.

The management theorist Henry Mintzberg found that managers have a preference for talking and doing, or what he called verbal interactions and action-oriented decisions. They aren't the type to stand still and take time to quietly reflect. They move—and they move quickly. The best managers, he said, combine this preference for movement with strong interpersonal skills and continuous information gathering, which leads them to possess keen insight into their work and make effective decisions.[2]

Eric and his assistant principals were everywhere: in the classrooms, the hallways, the cafeteria, and outside in front of the building as students arrived in the morning and when they were leaving for home in the afternoon, constantly complimenting students for their good behavior and praising the staff for helping students to improve. They were Mintzberg managers —always on the move and moving quickly—talking with students, staff, and parents, using their people skills, communicating and solving problems on the go. That's what it would take to turn their negative climate into a positive one.

It was challenging work and, at first, progress was slow. But Eric persevered and promised that when "Peace Days" finally started happening, they would celebrate. With the first peaceful day, Eric kept his promise. He sang for his staff and students. Before long, there were a couple of peaceful days. Now Eric and his assistant principals danced and lip synched to Aretha Franklin's "Respect." A few more uneventful days without bad behavior and he threw a make-your-own ice-cream sundae party for everyone. He made motivating speeches accompanied by PowerPoint slides with graphs showing how referrals to the principal's office and suspensions from school were dropping as test scores were rising. He bragged about his wonderful school to the parents and community organizations, and eventually it became the norm, rather than the exception, for there to be peaceful and productive days at school.

Eric Davis accomplished this school turn-around effort by using many strategies, but not least of which was the leaf he took from Elvis's book—**Be Daring and High Energy**.

While it's important to dare to try new ideas with high energy, it is also important to understand the climate you are operating within. You have to know what is really going on, before you dare to take a risk.

The M.I.T. scholar, Peter Senge, teaches us that every organization (a classroom, a school, a business) is a living organism. Both come from the root word "organ," which means part of a living thing that is adapted for a specific function. In nature, all living things seek a way to maintain balance so they can survive. Biologists call that balance *homeostasis*.

All of us, as living things, whether as individuals or as members of groups or organizations, experience forces that affect our balance; some forces that help advance our efforts and other forces that hinder our progress. Senge coined a name for this "inevitable interplay between growth and limiting processes." He called it the "dance of change."[3]

Before you, as a leader, try to make a change, especially a significant change that you think will really make a difference, you have to ask yourself: what balancing forces are at work? Which ones are going to assist you in moving forward? Which ones are going to push back and constrain you? If you don't understand where these forces come from and how they work and also how they are interrelated, then you are in for trouble.

Senge explains this idea with the metaphor of the hot room. Imagine that you walk into a really hot room (a classroom, an office) but you have no knowledge of how the heating system in the building works. The thermostat is set for 90 degrees. You feel like you're burning up. You can't work in these intolerable conditions. You can't even think. What should you do?

You decide to open a window to cool the room down. For a while it feels more comfortable, until the furnace comes on and makes it warmer again. So you open another window and the same thing happens. You feel cooler briefly and then the heat comes on and makes the room hotter again. You then decide to open every window, with the same result. You can't understand why your strategy isn't working. And yet, we, as outside observers, can see that there is no relief to be had by opening windows. Your method isn't working because the only thing that will produce results is starting by knowing how the thermostat works and how the furnace works and how they work together. Only by understanding these balancing forces can you make a decision that will produce the right kind of change and get the right result.[4]

The hot room metaphor plays out in schools and offices all the time. The Board of Education and the superintendent make a decision. They set a goal such as: we are going to increase the number of students taking more academically rigorous classes. One high-school principal hears the message and returns to his school and tells the guidance counselors and department heads to enroll more students in honors and advanced placement classes. At first they resist, fearing that some students who are not prepared for the difficult material will fail, but since the principal asked them to do it, they reluctantly begin to change students' schedules so that more of them will take the challenging courses.

But then some teachers begin to protest. "You're watering down my classes. You're lowering expectations. Our test scores and grades will fall." And then some students who are taking the more difficult courses for the first time want to drop out of them. "This class is too hard. The teacher doesn't help me." Some parents call the school to complain. "This is going to cause my child's grade point average to go down. How will she get into a good college?"

Before long, the driving forces of the Board of Education and the superintendent are coming up against the resisting forces of the teachers, students, and parents. The principal is caught in the middle. Where is the balance?

But what if the principal had studied the forces *before* making the change? What if he began by studying the environment and realizing that he couldn't get the full picture alone, and then asked his entire leadership team to study the situation with him? They might use a tool like a force-field analysis[5] designed to help leaders get a handle on the forces impacting an issue. After working together, they come to a consensus about what the environment is telling them, and only then does the leadership team make a change—a change designed to move ahead gradually, with an understanding of the school's need (as with any living organization), to maintain a balance—a balance in a new place, but a balance nonetheless. Now that they have decided to go in a new direction, they can put all of their energy into making the change work, implementing it to the best of their ability and carrying out their plans by bringing the teachers, students, and parents along with them. They still dared to take a risk and move. They still expended tremendous energy, but they did it after understanding the interrelated forces at work and being planful, strategic, and smart.

It's no surprise that every school I have seen that successfully increased the number of students taking more rigorous classes, and more importantly, the number of students who succeeded in passing the courses, accomplished it in this way, by assessing what Senge calls the growth and limiting processes and then daring to sail on, knowing they will sometimes face some strong head winds of resistance, tacking strategically when necessary, but determined to keep moving ahead.

It takes all of this to make real change—to make things better than they are now. It means that we, as leaders, have to move with the daring and high energy of Elvis, but we have to remember that we are always doing the "dance of change"— moving our organizations forward, learning the steps, and finding our new balance.

Diane Switlick was an assistant principal at a large middle school who understood the dance of change.[6] When she arrived at the school she saw students with learning and emotional disabilities in separate classes, with few, if any, opportunities to interact with other kids. Just as the Supreme Court's Brown vs. the Board of Education decision declared that, for race, "in the field of public education the doctrine of 'separate but equal' has no place,"[7] she knew that the same rule holds true for students with disabilities if they are segregated into self-contained classrooms and miss the chance to be in classes with all other students.

What Diane found was actually worse than just a school's scheduling problem. She saw that the students with disabilities were getting a lower-quality education. It wasn't the teachers' fault; they were doing the best they could under the circumstances. But a special education teacher responsible for teaching all subjects could rarely produce lessons of the same quality as teachers trained in a single subject who had the chance to hone their skills as they taught that subject all day.

The consequences for students were pretty dismal. The lessons in the special education classes weren't very stimulating. Tedious drill and practice worksheets were frequently assigned, and rarely did you see motivating, hands-on learning activities. The result was predictable: the students were bored, and as anyone who has ever worked in a school knows, boredom is the enemy, because bored students begin to misbehave. Where were the role models, the necessary critical mass of students who were motivated and interested in the lessons and who helped teachers create a positive classroom climate? They weren't in those self-contained classes of students with disabilities, which further deprived the classes of peers to help produce an academic atmosphere. Diane witnessed a steady stream of misbehaving students with disabilities being sent to the principal's office. No one was learning at a high level and no one was being successful, which only fed the students' self-perception that they had been put in these classes because they were too dumb to learn with other kids.

What Diane did next was daring. She asked the school's leadership team to consider a new model in which students with disabilities would be "mainstreamed" into regular classes wherever possible. Today we would call this idea "full inclusion," but at that time "mainstreaming" was the cutting-edge term.

Many of the leadership team members were horrified at the idea of teaching students identified as needing special education services. They said they didn't know how to teach them. "Wasn't this the special education teachers' jobs? Other schools don't have to do this. Why do we?"

We can already see the dance of change beginning to play out: the daring move forward—and the resisting forces pushing back.

Diane was ready for them. She had studied the ground she was operating on. To her, the environment appeared to have the potential for growth—this change could take place. Every chance she had she announced that this was the right thing to do, that there was a moral imperative here, that students with disabilities deserved a first-class education and that this was the way to bring it to them.

But the staff pushed back harder. Now it wasn't just the leadership team arguing that this change was happening too fast and without their consent; it was many teachers making the argument. They protested at their department meetings and at staff meetings. A steady stream of teachers dropped by the administrators' offices to register their concerns. They cared about all the students, they said, but they just didn't think the school was ready for such a drastic change—and besides, they had never been trained to deal with special education students, so it wasn't even fair to these kids with very special needs. What if they failed? Whose responsibility would that be? What if they misbehaved? Wouldn't that disrupt the education of all the other students?

Then word spread. Since schools are really communities, some of the teachers told the parents of their concerns and the parents began to ask whether this kind of change was really good for all children—and particularly their children. They sympathized with the parents of students with disabilities; they just didn't want "those" children in class with "their" children. After all, the kids in special education were below grade level. Would this mainstreaming plan be good for them? Or would they be frustrated since they couldn't do the higher-level work?

Diane and the other administrators had to re-think their plan. They were observing and listening and talking with everyone, and they realized that a full-scale rebellion against the initiative was beginning to build up steam. They had to take a closer look at the driving forces and the restraining forces. They knew some people were in favor of the change. Not everyone was against it. But they didn't have a critical mass to declare that this was going to be a school-wide change and carry the day. They realized that they had to go slower. They needed a plan that was less revolutionary and more incremental.

They decided to start with volunteer teams that Diane had personally recruited, just a few teachers paired up: a highly regarded English teacher working with a revered special education teacher; a respected math department head working as a team mate with a skilled special education teacher. Over the summer, Diane provided them with training about how to team teach and with planning time so that they could start the new school year as a genuine team with their own game plan.

As they began working with all kids, no matter whether a student had a disability or not, the other teachers watched—and what they saw surprised many of them. The teams of teachers found they really enjoyed working together, much more so than when they had worked alone. Most importantly, they found that no students suffered educationally from this experience, but the students with disabilities usually did much better than they had before. The number of students being sent to the principal's office declined dramatically. Maybe these teachers were on to something.

The second year there were more volunteers, most of whom Diane had once again personally recruited to give it a try. By the third year, so many teachers were team teaching that it was now possible to say that the school's philosophy had shifted. No longer was it assumed that students with disabilities should be educated in separate classes. Most of the time, everyone would learn together.

Every leader who inspires us possesses this quality. Not only do they dare to believe that improvement is possible, they study their environment to understand the forces at work, they talk with and listen to everyone to gather information, and they put all of their energy behind the new idea. The energy is contagious. It makes you want to join in and help move things forward. Daring, high-energy leaders often don't have to ask for their employees' help—people volunteer. We want to be with positive people who care so much they are willing to take the risk of stating publicly that they believe in our team, our office, our company—in us, and in our potential—and that together, we will continue to get better. It takes someone willing to take the first step to: **BE DARING AND HIGH ENERGY.**

Notes

1 Blake, William. *The Marriage of Heaven and Hell*, see http://www.good reads.com/quotes/122513-exuberance-is-beauty.

2 Mintzberg, Henry. 1989. *Mintzberg on Management*. Free Press. New York.

3 Senge, Peter, Kleiner, Art, Roberts, Charlotte, Ross, Richard, Roth, George, and Smith, Bryan. 1999. *The Dance of Change: A Fifth Discipline Resource*. Currency Doubleday. New York. P. 10.

4 Ibid. P. 559.

5 Lewin, K. 1943. Defining the "Field at a Given Time." *Psychological Review* 50: 292–310. Republished in *Resolving Social Conflicts and Field Theory in Social Science*. American Psychological Association, Washington, D.C., 1997.

6 Bradley, D., King-Sears, M., and Tessier-Switlick, D. 1997. An Inclusive Transition Experience, in *Teaching Students in Inclusive Settings: From Theory to Practice*. Allyn and Bacon. Boston, MA. Pp. 76–80.

7 Brown *v.* Board of Education 347 US 483 (1954).

8 See http://www.goodreads.com/quotes/294967-enthusiasm-is-one-of-the-most-powerful-engines-of-success.

Reflection Activity 10

Enthusiasm is one of the most powerful engines of success. When you do a thing, do it with all your might. Put your whole soul into it. Stamp it with your own personality. Be active, be energetic, be enthusiastic and faithful, and you will accomplish your object. Nothing great was ever achieved without enthusiasm.

Ralph Waldo Emerson,[8]
American essayist and poet

Every great musician performs with enthusiasm as does anyone who has ever accomplished anything important. We respect athletes when we can say they "left it all on the field." We are inspired by leaders who dared to "go all out" and who "put their whole heart and soul" into trying to make their organizations, and us, better than we were, and even better than we thought we could be.

Mark Amberg dared to accept every child into his chorus. Eric Davis dared to believe peace days could lead to peace weeks and months and transform his school's climate. Diane Switlick dared to change the way students with disabilities were educated. They each took a risk and then put all of their energy into turning their risk into reality.

Facing a challenge with a new idea and being energetic isn't always enough. It also calls for what we learned from Henry Mintzberg—that we need to use our energy to constantly communicate with people as we collect information. It requires what Peter Senge teaches us, that we need to understand the interplay of driving and resisting forces so we can find our new balance in the "dance of change." Then we can be planful and strategic as well as enthusiastic. It takes all of these qualities to **Be Daring and High Energy** in order to realize lofty goals and accomplish great things.

Who do you know who has demonstrated **Leadership Lesson 10: Be Daring and High Energy**? What did they do and say? Be as specific as possible. What did you learn from them that you want to apply to your own life and work?

_____

_____

_____

_____

_____

_____

_____

_____

_____

_____

_____

_____

_____

_____

_____

Reflect further by doing the self-rating scales below. If this leadership lesson is one you have just started using, you are at the beginning phase. If you are using this leadership lesson regularly, you are now at the practicing phase. Like expert musicians we need to commit to practicing these lessons for our entire careers and lives. When you have mastered this leadership lesson and incorporated it naturally into your repertoire, you have reached the leading level.

Rate yourself using this scale. Mark a place on the line that represents *your* current state on **Leadership Lesson 10: Be Daring and High Energy**.

1	2	3	4	5

Beginning	Practicing	Leading

Rate your team, department, school, office, business, or organization using this scale. Mark a place on the line that represents *your group*'s current state on **Leadership Lesson 10: Be Daring and High Energy**.

1	2	3	4	5

Beginning	Practicing	Leading

What commitment will you and the people with whom you work make to fulfill this leadership characteristic? How can you incorporate the leadership lesson of **Being Daring and High Energy** into your life and work? What concrete action steps will you take? What will be the sequence? What timeline will you follow?

Commitment:

_____

_____

_____

_____

_____

_____

Action Steps	Person(s) Responsible	Timeline

Carlos Santana

LESSON 11:
Unify

Carlos Santana live in Hamburg, November 1973
Credit: Heinrich Klaffs, www.flickr.com/photos/heiner1947/4484760723. Permission from CC-BY-SA. Entered public domain 2010.

CARLOS SANTANA was born in Mexico. His father was a famous Mariachi violinist and Carlos first took up the violin when he was five years old, following in his father's footsteps. The instrument he is known for, the guitar, came into his life a few years later when his family moved to Tijuana, and he was strongly influenced by American blues guitarists like B. B. King, who he heard on the radio.

In 1961 he moved to San Francisco and later formed the Santana Blues Band, which was unusual because it was diverse, with members who were Latino, African American, and white. Together they created a Latin-blues-based sound that found a loyal audience in the Bay Area. Later they played on the Ed Sullivan Show, held concerts all over the world and, in 1969, gave a ground-breaking performance at the original Woodstock Festival.

In **Leadership Lesson 4: Be Eclectic**, we learned that George Gershwin wrote in many styles and reached different audiences, just as leaders need to use a range of strategies in order to successfully motivate the people they are responsible for and to move their organizations forward. Carlos Santana takes eclecticism to another level—a world level. In a profile for the 2013 Kennedy Center Honors, *Washington Post* writer David Montgomery put it this way: "True, he was born in Autlan de Navarro, Mexico, and honed his guitar chops in the streets and dives of Tijuana. But the identity that matters most to Santana—his artistic and spiritual self—is bigger, embracing roots from Mali to Haiti to Cuba to the Mississippi Delta."[1]

Beyond eclecticism, there is something even more inclusive happening in Santana's music. George Gershwin combined European and African American music to compose the opera *Porgy and Bess*. Similarly, Carlos Santana has created an extensive melding of many musical styles and cultures, including Latin music and other traditions. The biography on his website describes his music: "His signature sound—fusing rock, jazz, blues, soul, Latin idioms, multi-cultural genres and more—is as unique as it is instantly identifiable. With his lifetime of music and achievement, Santana has become a cultural event—transcending genre, crossing cultures—creating the music that has become the soundtrack for the world."[2]

The idea of synthesizing various ideas into something new is the leadership lesson we learn from Carlos Santana:

UNIFY

The Lesson Goes to School:
How Educators Can Unify

Producing a unified and clearly recognizable sound in music that fuses different influences and traditions is not so different from the challenge a leader faces when attempting to achieve a unified and clear vision and mission for a diverse group of people working together. Whether they are students in a classroom, staff in a school, players on a team, or employees in a company or non-profit organization, people long for a feeling of unity and clarity of purpose.

Synergy is the term (from Greek, meaning "working together") most often used to describe the result that occurs when multiple elements produce an effect different from or greater than the sum of their individual effects. Or, as we often say: the whole is greater than the sum of its parts. When those multiple elements include people with their own unique thoughts, feelings, goals, and needs, it can be a test for any leader.

Stephen Covey felt so strongly about the power of synergy that he made it his sixth habit in his bestselling *The 7 Habits of Highly Effective People.*[3] He describes synergy as creative cooperation and reminds us that it requires open-mindedness to the "mental, emotional and psychological differences among people."[4] In a band, side men are the musicians who are the support players, not the stars. Trumpet player and side man Bill Ortiz said about playing with Carlos Santana: "Most artists who have reached this level of success in the music industry, when they perform, it's generally all about them. One of the great things about him as a bandleader is he really values the input of his side people."[5] This type of open-mindedness helped Santana **Unify** his music and can help all leaders **Unify** their organizations.

The literature on leadership is filled with recommendations about the need for leaders to have their own vision—to be visionary leaders. But this emphasis on the leader's personal image of an idealized future misses a crucial point. I have often had the experience of sitting on an interview panel with students, staff, and parents who were selecting a new principal. Someone inevitably asks the candidates to describe their vision for the school. The candidates typically answer the question with broad generic statements about their commitment to every student achieving his or her potential. A better answer would be for a candidate to say something like this:

> I have some core values that are central to who I am, such as my belief that every child deserves the best education possible. However, a vision for our school is something we are going to build together, representing everyone's views and with everyone's input. People want many different things from their school. We need to make sure that our vision meets all of those needs. I am committed to working with everyone to make a unified vision for our school—one that we can all believe in and one that we will work hard to achieve together.

Leaders who want to **Unify** their teams know that the vision has to be created collaboratively. A teacher who holds the value that his classroom should be a safe place for students knows he has a much better chance of creating that kind of nurturing classroom climate if his students have some say about the class rules. For this reason, William Glasser, the founder of Reality Therapy, recommends that teachers hold regular class meetings in which students share their thoughts and feelings about how the class operates.[6] A principal who holds the value that the most important work of a school is teaching and learning knows she has a much better chance of creating that kind of academic school environment if the teachers and other staff have meaningful participation in the school's operation. Thomas Marzano and his research colleagues found that one of a principal's responsibilities which has the highest correlation with student academic achievement is *input*—"the extent to which the principal involves teachers in the design and implementation of important decisions and policies."[7]

Carole Working became the principal of Quince Orchard High School, a large suburban high school with a history of solid achievement by almost any measure: high promotion and graduation rates, impressive SAT scores, successful sports teams, and positive surveys of parent satisfaction. When Carole examined her school's data she discovered that, at the end of each year, there was a small group of students who didn't graduate. How could she **Unify** her entire school on behalf of these at-risk students? She found a way: by making it personal.

Carole knew she was lucky because the school had a very committed staff. They were a large staff of over 200 and a diverse staff in every way: by race, culture, gender, background, education, training, and beliefs. Now she had to rally them to this one cause. Every student should graduate, she believed, and if a few students didn't walk across the stage to receive their diplomas, the school should have done everything humanly possible on their behalf. She was sure that if the staff felt that they knew these young people and saw the impact on their lives, they would want to take action.

She began, as most administrators do, by sharing the data with the staff. But data analysis, to most people, seems like a cold process. It involves analyzing numbers and looking for mathematical trends. It doesn't feel warm and human. Teachers go into teaching because they enjoy working with children—not because they like examining graphs. Carole decided she needed to warm up the cold data by inserting the students' photographs. Every time an administrator, counselor, or teacher pulled up a report about a student on their computer, the screen not only showed the student's grades, test scores, and attendance, it also displayed the student's picture. Now it wasn't just a page of numbers; it was a real student whose record was before them.

Then Carole made a more dramatic move and she did it in an unlikely setting. In most schools, teachers find staff meetings to be tedious affairs to endure. An hour after school spent in the school's library or cafeteria in which exhausted teachers try to give the appearance of paying attention to beleaguered administrators telling them irrelevant information while surreptitiously grading their never-ending stack of student papers. Carole, on the advice of a colleague, tried a new approach called the Rolling Staff Meeting. Instead of one meeting held after school in the traditional way, she held seven small staff meetings for about 20 teachers at a time. Each period of the school day, a new

20 teachers would come into an unused classroom to have a meeting with their principal. The setting was more intimate, the presentations by the administrators were more conversational, and there was more dialogue—more give and take.

The dramatic move came during the last five minutes. Hanging on the blackboard were three posters. Each poster contained small photographs of students with their names printed beneath them. Carole said to her staff:

> We are a really great school. We owe a lot of that to you because you work very hard, you have tremendous expertise, and you are extremely committed. Almost all of our students graduate and then go on to college. Many of them earn scholarships and have wonderful opportunities in life. But every year there are a small number of students who don't graduate. We need to work together to figure out what to do to help them. On the board behind me are pictures of our students who may not graduate this year. Although they are seniors, they may not have the grades or the credits to pass. If they don't, there will be a question about whether they'll drop out. I'm worried about them. I know you are worried, too. Together, let's find some new ways to help them turn their situations around.

When she had finished, there was silence. Carole thanked them for coming and wished them a good rest of the day. Then we saw something happen that surprised us. Although you would have expected the teachers to be in a rush to leave since the bell was about to ring and they needed to get ready for their next classes, most of them stayed for a few minutes. They crowded around the blackboard and began looking at the pictures—not casually viewing them like people sometimes do in an art gallery, but closely examining them and commenting to each other:

"I had him in ninth grade. I thought he was an average student. I never thought he would fall so far behind."

"She was in my sophomore biology class. I remember she had attendance issues."

"I think he was in special ed. He had trouble staying focused and taking notes."

"She just got here a few years ago from El Salvador. She was behind in her vocabulary and reading comprehension, but she was very motivated. I wonder what happened."

The meeting had just ended and the conversation among the teachers had already begun. It continued for the next few weeks as they considered what to do about the kids they recognized in the photographs, who they had taught, who they knew, and who they worried were going to fail to graduate.

Now that they were becoming **Unified** about a problem that needed to be solved, they started making some decisions. They began calling parents early on when they had concerns about a student's progress. They started spending more time individually tutoring those who needed it the most. The heads of departments closely monitored students' grades and coached teachers about other ways to reach the kids who weren't learning.

The initial results were promising enough to make everyone believe it would be possible to save even more of their students. Even when teachers took the first step of calling home once each marking period, it proved to be a powerful enough approach to keep some students from failing a class. In time, the staff made plans to put other strategies in place and the results were even better.

Carole used her belief that every student should graduate and have access to life's opportunities as a way to **Unify** a large diverse staff around that mission. She made it personal. Because when it's personal, it really matters and you want to do something about it.

Unity comes easier when everyone has a similar perspective and agrees easily. Although similar perspectives don't necessarily lead to new or better ideas and solutions. For real productivity, you need some conflict, or at least some exchange of views. Researchers in the field of organizational behavior discovered that in the most effective groups, the members first encourage discussion of their disagreements as part of the problem-solving process, before trying to agree on solutions, whereas ineffective groups rush to agreement in an effort to get the task done as quickly as possible.[8] If you want to achieve unity of purpose, it's much better to take the slower route, understanding that the conflict between the group's members is much more likely to take you to an actual solution that people will get excited about and **Unified** about supporting.

Just because everyone cooperates doesn't necessarily mean that the group is being productive. We have all seen people who "go along to get along" without putting their hearts and souls into a project. For real collaboration to take place, everyone has to feel psychologically safe[9] to take the risk of expressing their opinions, especially when they believe that their views aren't held by the majority or by the leader. Psychologists who study group dynamics have found that a shared belief that a team is safe for interpersonal risk taking is key to innovation, learning from mistakes, and employee engagement. You can tell from the trumpet player's comments that Santana made his musicians feel safe enough to offer their best ideas: "he really values the input of his side people."[10] And as we learned in **Leadership Lesson 5: Lead by Participating,** openness to his musician's contributions was one of the factors in Duke Ellington's success. After all, it was Duke's collaborator Billy Strayhorn's "Take the 'A' Train" that became the band's signature song. It's tough to stick your neck out. It takes courage. But it's a little easier if the leader has created a safe environment for people to express their views.

Whether you are a principal like Carole Working trying to **Unify** a large diverse staff to better meet students' various needs or a musician like Carlos Santana fusing many traditions to **Unify** a diverse band's ground-breaking new sound, the best approach for any leader is to make people feel psychologically safe, accept a wide variety of ideas and perspectives, involve people in decision making, and create your new vision and direction together.

Notes

1 Montgomery, D. 2013. Saluting a Singular Guitar Stylist. *Washington Post*. December 8. P. E3.

2 See http://www.santana.com/frameset2.html (the official site of Carlos Santana and the Santana Band, Biography).

3 Covey, S. 1989. *The 7 Habits of Highly Effective People*. Simon and Schuster. New York.

4 See https://www.stephencovey.com/7habits/7habits-habit6.php.

5 Montgomery, D. 2013. Saluting a Singular Guitar Stylist. *Washington Post*. December 8. P. E3.

6 Glasser, W. 1969. *Schools without Failure*. Harper and Row. New York.

7 Marzano, R. J., Waters, T., and McNulty, B. A. 2005. *School Leadership that Works*. ASCD. Alexandria, VA.

8 Studies by Jay Hall reported in Buchanan, D. and Huczynski, A. 1997. *Organizational Behavior*. 3rd edition. Prentice Hall. Englewood Cliffs, NJ. P. 276.

9 Edmondson, Amy. 1999. Psychological Safety and Learning Behavior in Work Teams. *Administrative Science Quarterly* 44(2): 350–83, doi: 10.2307/2666999. Retrieved April 14, 2014 from: http://www.iacmr.org/Conferences/WS2011/Submission_XM/Participant/Readings/Lecture9B_Jing/Edmondson,%20ASQ%201999.pdf.

10 Montgomery, D. 2013. Saluting a Singular Guitar Stylist. *Washington Post*. December 8. P. E3.

11 Dumas, Alexandre. 1844. *The Three Musketeers*. Modern Library. New York.

12 NPR Music. Retrieved April 14, 2014 from: http://www.npr.org/2012/04/24/151294671/classical-rock-star-bell-takes-on-conducting.

Reflection Activity 11

All for one and one for all!

Alexandre Dumas, author,
The Three Musketeers[11]

In an interview on National Public Radio, Grammy Award-winning Violinist Joshua Bell said, "I mean, the great secret is that an orchestra can actually play without a conductor at all. Of course, a great conductor will have a concept and will help them play together and unify them."[12]

Carlos Santana unified his diverse band and his unique music by fusing many traditions into a new sound. Joshua Bell would have said he is the leader with a concept that helps his band play together. Principal Carole Working had a concept too. She unified her large, diverse high-school staff by focusing on the students in danger of not graduating and making the issue personal. Both leaders helped their group feel the energy in the rallying cry: "All for one and one for all!" This is the power of being unified.

Psychologists who study organizational behavior know that there are ways to unify a group and help it become its most productive. The members need to feel psychologically safe to contribute without fear or anxiety and the leader needs to have an open-minded attitude that invites everyone's contributions. Then the vision is not originated solely by the leader; it becomes everyone's vision because everyone had input into creating it.

Who do you know who has demonstrated **Leadership Lesson 11: Unify**? What did they do and say? Be as specific as possible. What did you learn from them that you want to apply to your own life and work?

_____

_____

_____

_____

_____

_____

_____

_____

_____

_____

_____

_____

_____

_____

_____

_____

Reflect further by doing the self-rating scales below. If this leadership lesson is one you have just started using, you are at the beginning phase. If you are using this leadership lesson regularly, you are now at the practicing phase. Like expert musicians we need to commit to practicing these lessons for our entire careers and lives. When you have mastered this leadership lesson and incorporated it naturally into your repertoire, you have reached the leading level.

Rate yourself using this scale. Mark a place on the line that represents _your_ current state on **Leadership Lesson 11: Unify**.

1	2	3	4	5
Beginning		Practicing		Leading

Rate your team, department, school, office, business, or organization using this scale. Mark a place on the line that represents *your group*'s current state on **Leadership Lesson 11: Unify**.

1	2	3	4	5

Beginning	Practicing	Leading

What commitment will you and the people with whom you work make to your fulfillment of this leadership characteristic? How can you incorporate the leadership lesson **Unify** into your life and work? What concrete action steps will you take? What will be the sequence? What timeline will you follow?

Commitment:

_____

_____

_____

_____

_____

_____

Action Steps	Person(s) Responsible	Timeline

Legend: The Beatles

LESSON 12:
Use Teamwork

The Beatles
Credit: Photofest

TRY THIS LITTLE BEATLES TRIVIA QUIZ.

1. Who was the funny one?
2. Who was the quiet one?
3. Who was the edgy, intellectual one?
4. Who was the cute one?[1]

Everyone who grew up in the 1960s knows the names of the Beatles. Although we recognize a lot of other bands from that era (the Rolling Stones, the Animals, Jefferson Airplane, the Doors), except for their lead singers, I can't name all the members of the groups; can you? Yet we know the names of each of the Beatles and even a little about John, Paul, George, and Ringo.

We remember them because they were all essential contributors to the band's sound and personality. Each one helped the Beatles become what they were, not just a famous singer with some back-up musicians, but the "Fab Four"—the group we loved, and whose lives we followed for years, even after they broke up. This is the reason I chose them to illustrate the leadership principle:

USE TEAMWORK

The Lesson Goes to School:
How Educators Can Use Teamwork

We have all heard the saying: "The whole is greater than the sum of its parts." For leadership, we could rephrase it: "The leadership team is greater than the sum of its members."

I once knew a high-school principal named Dr. Benjamin Marlin who had lunch with his administrative team of assistant principals every day. In that time together, they talked about many topics—how to handle tough student behavior cases, challenging staff problems, and difficult parent issues. Years later, I was talking with a human resources specialist who said that of the close to 200 principals in the district, Ben had the greatest number of assistant principals promoted to principalships, and every one of them cited those lunch meetings as the source of their greatest professional development. Each one then carried the lesson forward and formed cohesive administrative teams in their own schools by meeting frequently and working closely together.

Anyone who has worked in a school or in a business or non-profit organization has, at some time, taken the Myers-Briggs Type Indicator Inventory,[2] or some other personality survey to identify your preferred operating style. Are you an introvert or an extrovert? Are you thinking or feeling? Are you sensing or intuitive? Are you perceiving or judgmental? In addition to being useful for self-reflection, these tools also contain an important teamwork lesson: to make good decisions, we need as many of the various personality types sitting around the leadership table as possible.

Considering teams in terms of how they think, we can look at intelligence like Harvard psychologist Howard Gardner did.[3] He rejected a narrow view of intelligence and instead defined it as "the capacity to solve problems." Instead of thinking about IQ as the knowledge and skills assessed on college readiness tests like the SAT, he developed a theory of multiple intelligences—identifying different types of intelligences, some not usually tapped or valued in school or the workplace. This idea, that there are different ways of being smart, came home to me in a very personal way.

My wife and I have two sons, Dan and Ben. Dan is about two years older than Ben. When they were in elementary school, it was clear that they had different learning styles. Ben loved school; Dan hated it. Ben was very verbal; Dan avoided speaking whenever possible. Ben loved stories and learned to read and write early; Dan loved strategy games and could beat anyone at checkers and chess at an early age.

One day we were driving our big Suburban station wagon with both boys and their friends in the back seats. We decided to stop by the supermarket to pick up some ice cream. When we pulled into the parking lot, we all got out of the car and closed the doors—click, click, click . . . BANG! Three doors closed, but one slammed back open. Dan's friend's door, the one behind the driver's, wouldn't close. I said, "Try it again." The boy shoved the door harder this time, but it banged back open again. I tried it with the same result.

I have a Ph.D. and I didn't have a clue about where to start to fix the door. My wife was an English major and she had no idea. Ben, who flourished in school, just shrugged. But Dan, who struggled in school, silently kneeled down so the broken door's lock was at his eye level and peered into the mechanism, studying it. He took a few steps forward and kneeled down in front of my door and stared into it. Then he went back to the broken door, kneeled down again, and like a doctor calling for his scalpel said, "Dad, give me your pen." He took the pen and put it into the lock and pushed something that made a metallic snap. He stood up and closed the door, which clicked shut just like the others.

Not one of us who had traditional school smarts knew what to do. The boy with different kinds of intelligence, who had other approaches to solving problems, figured it out.

When we're on a team and putting our heads together to try to solve a problem, we can make good use of all the multiple intelligences to help us find a solution. We need people with strengths in logic and mathematics and language, as well as those who can construct abstract mental models. We need people with interpersonal skills and those who are more reflective about themselves. We need the global thinkers and the linear thinkers. We need the ones with strong data analysis skills and, as we learn from psychologist and journalist Daniel Goleman,[4] we also need those with heightened emotional intelligence who can understand their own feelings as well as other people's emotions and can use this understanding to guide their thinking and actions.

We need everybody's observations and insights. When a team draws on different perspectives, it's a better team. Paul McCartney once explained that every Beatles' song was submitted to the group for approval. Each Beatle reviewed it and added his own ideas to make the song better. The whole group had to come to agreement before the song was recorded.[5] That is what effective teams do.

When team mates experience that kind of collegiality, it impacts both the quality of their professional relationships and their productivity. In the most successful schools, staff members are true colleagues who talk about their work to make it better, says researcher Judith Warren Little.[6] But it is not always easy to build these relationships.

Anita Prince and Margy Hall were elementary teachers who I recruited to lead sixth-grade teams at Gaithersburg Middle School (the same school we read about in Chapter 10 where assistant principal Diane Switlick exemplified the leadership trait of **Being Daring and High Energy** when she convinced the staff to include students with special needs). I asked Anita and Margy to work at the middle school, not only because they had the reputation of being excellent teachers, but because we were facing a huge challenge, converting an intermediate school for 1,200 seventh and eighth graders into a middle school for students in grades six, seven, and eight. Now we would be organized, not by individual academic departments like a typical junior high or high school, but by interdisciplinary teams with each team composed of an English teacher, a math teacher, a science teacher, and a social studies teacher, and sometimes a special education teacher or teacher of English for students new to learning the language. We needed to make a shift from a focus on individual courses taught by individual teachers who operated primarily in isolation, except for their affiliation with a department, to a focus on teamwork.

Margy and Anita went to work. They named their teams after Maryland symbols: the Chesapeakes, the Orioles. They asked the teachers to plan special events together—field trips, student recognition assemblies. They developed team spirit and team rules for student behavior. They emphasized Chesapeake and Oriole pride in everything they did. They even held parent conferences as a team so that parents could meet all their children's teachers and talk about what their children needed.

At first, some teachers didn't like the new direction. After all, working together as a team takes time, time that could be spent making lesson plans and grading papers, and teachers never have enough time to get all their work done. It takes a lot of time for teams to talk things over, to figure out how they will operate, how they will make decisions, how they will analyze their students' achievement needs, and how they will address them.

It's not easy work, even without the natural human dynamics that take place as people sometimes disagree and have to learn how to cooperate and get along. Management consultant Patrick Lencioni[7] describes all the typical dysfunctional behaviors of teams we witnessed at first: absence of trust, fear of conflict, lack of commitment, avoidance of accountability, and inattention to results.

Eventually, Margy and Anita did build teams in which the teachers trusted each other and shared their ideas, even if it meant they had to work out disagreements. They made decisions and plans together and committed to carrying them out. They held each other accountable and took pride in their achievements and in their collective results. Their teams eventually became what the educator Rick DuFour[8] calls *professional learning communities* with a shared vision and values, a focus on their students' learning, and a real culture of trust, respect, and collaboration.

And what were their results? Students began feeling that they were not just members of *any* team, their first loyalty was to *their* team—even more than to their school, which was all right with us. What we were seeing was what some people call the "Cheers"[9] effect—the positive results you see when you're in a place, as the show's theme song says, "where everybody knows your name."[10]

If you are a student, how do you act when you are part of a team where the teachers really know you and care about you? Your grades go up and you have no need to misbehave. The Chesapeakes and the Orioles saw student achievement rise and student misbehavior fall dramatically. Within two years, the seventh- and eighth-grade departments had transformed into teams working just as cooperatively. Within five years, the state of Maryland recognized the school twice for making such significant gains in student achievement.

In their insightful book, *Why Teams Don't Work*,[11] Harvey Robbins and Michael Finley tell the story of William Deming, the statistician who later became a celebrated management theorist and consultant. After World War II, Deming contributed many of the ideas that turned Japanese corporations around and helped create the Japanese economic miracle. After the war, the Japanese had no raw materials, no technology, and no infrastructure, but he observed that they did have people who were culturally disposed to work together. When Deming was later asked what he had learned from the Japanese, he didn't hesitate even for a moment to answer, "People are important."[12]

Deming was right—people ARE important—but to form a great team you have to remember that you don't want everyone to be the same. The easiest mistake is to hire everyone who thinks as we do—because "we're on the same wavelength." We need some new thoughts and some new ideas, to stretch us so that we become better, but more importantly because we want our schools and organizations to be the most innovative and successful schools and organizations possible. That takes a lot of different strengths, more than any one of us possesses alone. The Beatles were a great band, a great team, largely because they weren't all the same but because they brought different talents to the table, or in their case, into the recording studio.

When members of a team are all different and all have their own strengths, sometimes you face the problem of a lack of cohesiveness, an inability to work together productively. Columnist Thomas Friedman of the *New York Times* drew a lesson from the 2008 Summer Olympics. He said, "The American men's basketball team did poorly in the last Olympics (2004) because it could not play as a team. Our stars were beaten by inferior players with better teamwork. Our basketball team learned its lesson."[13] (It certainly did; that year the Re-Deem Team took home the gold.) You could argue that it took Mike Krzyzewski, the incredible Duke coach, to forge that kind of group commitment out of uniquely talented individuals. That's what great leaders do—they **Use Teamwork** as one of the keys to succeeding.

There is also a second way to think about teamwork: the need to build a team outside of your school, department, or office. Dr. Jerry Marco retired after a career spanning over 30 years as one of the most successful high-school principals his district had ever known. He could be a model for many effective leadership practices, but the one I want to highlight here is the way he built a sense of team beyond his school.

When Jerry arrived at a meeting of high-school principals, he would often be carrying a stack of papers. If he found a useful research article he would distribute copies of it at the meeting, assuming that he ought to share anything of value he came across. If he had arranged for the appearance of a prestigious guest speaker at his school, all of his colleagues were invited to come. If you were new to your job, he would take you aside and offer to help you with anything you needed. I took him up on the offer and sometimes emailed him asking for advice. By the end of the day he always responded with a thoughtful reply, either supplying the answer or making a suggestion or providing a lead about how to find the information I needed. Who knows how many other people he was simultaneously mentoring, even while running his own large high school, always finding the time for each of us?

Most memorable were Jerry's emails just before each major holiday. Of course, they wished us a happy holiday and a healthy and restful break. But more importantly, he always asked us to reflect on what was really important to us—our families—and he urged us to leave the work on our desks ("It'll be there when you get back") and to make time for our loved ones. He asked us to remember that we were doing important work and that we were in it together, but there were times to leave the work at work and enjoy our families and replenish our bodies and spirits. No one who ever received these messages ever forgot them. In this way, Jerry built a team outside of his school; a team of colleagues throughout the system who Jerry respected and cared about and who felt the same way about him, and so we became a more cohesive group who could depend on one another. That is teamwork, too.

A coda: years after Jerry retired, I was sitting in a restaurant with Benjamin OuYang, a young man who had just been promoted to become the principal of a middle school. Ben saw Jerry across the room, sitting in a booth with his wife having lunch, and said, with reverence in his voice, "There's Dr. Marco. I need to go say hello. I'm only a principal because of him. I was teaching in his school and he told me that I should become an administrator because he saw something in me that I didn't see in myself."

The new young principal rushed over to Dr. Marco, with me trailing behind, and, when he got there, thanked Jerry for encouraging him and then told him the good news about his promotion—wanting his mentor to share the happiness he felt, but also the credit for the accomplishment. When you **Use Teamwork**, sometimes you only find out years later about the mark it made on your team mates, the meaning it had for them, and the long-term results it produced.

Notes

1   Answers to the Beatles trivia quiz: 1. Ringo; 2. George; 3. John; 4. Paul.
2   Briggs Myers, I. 1980. *Gifts Differing*. Consulting Psychologists Press. Mountain View, CA.
3   Gardner, H. 1983; 1993. *Frames of Mind: The Theory of Multiple Intelligences*. Basic Books. New York.
4   Goleman, D. 1995. *Emotional Intelligence*. Bantam Books. New York.
5   See www.colbertnation.com/the-colbert.../june-12–2013.
6   Warren Little, Judith. 1981. *School Success and Staff Development in Urban Desegregated Schools*. Center for Action Research. Los Angeles, CA; and 1982. Norms of Collegiality and Experimentation. In Barth, Roland S. 2006. Improving Relationships within the School House. *Educational Leadership* 63(6): 8–13.
7   Lencioni, P. 2002. *The Five Dysfunctions of a Team*. Jossey-Bass. San Francisco, CA.
8   Dufour, R. and Eaker, R. 1998. *Professional Learning Communities at Work: Best Practices for Enhancing Student Achievement*. Solution Tree Press. Bloomington, IN.
9   *Cheers!* American sitcom (1982–93). Produced by Charles/Burrows/ Charles Productions in association with Paramount Network Television for NBC and created by the team of James Burrows, Glen Charles, and Les Charles.
10 "Where Everybody Knows Your Name" (1982). Composed by Portnoy, Gary and Angelo, Judy Hart. See www.garyportnoy.com.
11 Robbins, H. and Finley, M. 1995. *Why Teams Don't Work*. Audio book 1997. High Bridge Company. Minneapolis, MN.
12 Ibid. Also see Walton, M. 1986. *The Deming Management Method*. Perigee Books. New York.
13 Freidman. T. 2008. Melting Pot Meets Great Wall. *New York Times*. August 24. P. 10.
14 On the "Feminine Revolution." 1972. *Sundance Magazine*, http:// archive.8m.net/lennon&ono.htm.

15 Gertner, Jon. 2012. *The Idea Factory: Bell Labs and the Great Age of American Innovation*. Penguin Press. New York (as cited in Isaacson, Walter. 2012. Inventing the Future. *New York Times*. April 8. P. 20).
16 Maslow, A. 1954. *Motivation and Personality*. Harper. New York.

Reflection Activity 12

A dream you dream alone is only a dream. A dream you
dream together is reality.
                                    Yoko Ono and John Lennon[14]

When principal Ben Marlin brought his assistant principals together for lunch and conversation each day, his goal wasn't only to solve day-to-day problems. He was also developing a shared vision about how all people should be treated at their school. Together they were creating a new reality. By modeling generosity and sharing, principal Jerry Marco was attempting to build an improved spirit of cohesion among all of the principals in the entire school district.

We learned from personality inventories like the Myers-Briggs and researchers like Howard Gardner and writers like Daniel Goleman that we should value all the different strengths and talents that members bring to a team. The examples in **Lesson 12: Use Teamwork** originate in schools, but this approach applies to any organization.

In his book *The Idea Factory: Bell Labs and the Great Age of American Innovation*, Jon Gertner explains how this collaborative organization produced so many important industrial innovations. He maintained that, "The lesson of Bell Labs is that most feats of sustained innovation cannot and do not occur in an iconic garage or the workshop of an ingenious inventor. They occur when people of diverse talents and mind-sets and expertise are brought together, preferably in close physical proximity where they can have frequent meetings and serendipitous encounters."[15]

Margy Hall and Anita Prince made their six grade teaching teams into collaborative units in which teachers with diverse strengths and interests enjoyed sharing ideas, learning from each other, and improving their students' achievement.

There is a desire in all of us to be part of something bigger than ourselves. The psychologist Abraham Maslow[16] taught generations of college students that there is a hierarchy of needs, and right in the middle of his iconic triangle model is the need for affiliation—for belonging—not as basic as the need for food and shelter, but absolutely essential before a person can consider intellectual pursuits like learning. Well-coordinated and cohesive teams fulfill this human need and leaders who **Use Teamwork** are caring about their co-workers at the same time as they are helping them to become contributors to a group that can produce more than any of them can accomplish on their own. The dream they dream together is not only reality, but also their vision for the future.

Who do you know who has demonstrated **Leadership Lesson 12: Use Teamwork**? What did they do and say? Be as specific as possible. What did you learn from them that you want to apply to your own life and work?

_____

_____

_____

_____

_____

_____

_____

_____

_____

_____

_____

_____

_____

_____

_____

_____

Reflect further by doing the self-rating scales below. If this leadership lesson is one you have just started using, you are at the beginning phase. If you are using this leadership lesson regularly, you are now at the practicing phase. Like expert musicians we need to commit to practicing these lessons for our entire careers and lives. When you have mastered this leadership lesson and incorporated it naturally into your repertoire, you have reached the leading level.

Rate yourself using this scale. Mark a place on the line that represents *your* current state on **Leadership Lesson 12: Use Teamwork**.

1	2	3	4	5
Beginning		Practicing		Leading

Rate your team, department, school, office, business, or organization using this scale. Mark a place on the line that represents *your group*'s current state on **Leadership Lesson 12: Use Teamwork**.

1	2	3	4	5
Beginning		Practicing		Leading

What commitment will you and the people with whom you work make to fulfill this leadership characteristic? How can you incorporate the leadership lesson of **Using Teamwork** into your life and work? What concrete action steps will you take? What will be the sequence? What timeline will you follow?

Commitment:

_____

_____

_____

_____

_____

_____

Action Steps	Person(s) Responsible	Timeline

The Temptations

LESSON 13:
Move Together

The Temptations
Credit: Photofest

WHEN YOU WATCH the Temptations perform, you think of perfect harmony and movement in complete synchronicity. They are so smooth, so elegant, so together. You only need to listen to the beginning bass beats of "My Girl" and you immediately recognize one of the Temptations' biggest hits. You want to snap your fingers, sing along, and start to dance. If the Beatles teach us to work as a team, the Temptations teach us that our team needs to

MOVE TOGETHER

The Lesson Goes to School: How Educators Can Move Together

As with the other leadership lessons, it sounds easy, and when it's done right, it looks effortless. But appearances can be misleading. Just like the Temptations' unified and inspired dancing, moving together takes a lot of practice.

In the very best schools I've worked with, there is a sense that everyone is in it together and the school is moving ahead, each person playing a part. Not everyone is doing the same thing or in the same way. But they are all contributing and coordinating parts of the whole. Ask any sports team and they will tell you that they feel this way when the team is playing at its best.

When I was a high-school principal, the best compliment our school ever received came from a George Washington University professor who was researching staff development in our county's schools. He told us that we had the most significant results. He had never seen anything like it. When he randomly selected teachers to interview, they could all tell him what we had agreed upon as the parts of an effective lesson. "They all knew them!" he said in amazement. "That, in itself, is unusual. But the surprising part is that they all, without any prompting, voluntarily told me that they agreed with them."

That's what it means to **Move Together**.

Achieving Temptations-style synchronicity requires a few key steps. First, everyone has to play a part in deciding where the school is going, setting clear and reasonable goals. Just as important, it is deciding how we are going to move forward, and at what speed, and with what types of support. It is crucial to use an inclusive process[1] to provide a structure that involves everyone. *You have to be involved with others before you can move with others.*

The social psychologist Kurt Lewin transformed the way we think about how people interact with each other. He maintained that being a group doesn't depend on the similarity or differences of its members. What is important, however, is whether they feel that their fate is interdependent. The best way to feel this type of connectedness is to set group goals and realize that you are dependent on each other to achieve your goals.[2]

Support for the idea of involving people in decision making as a prerequisite to effectively helping them **Move Together** as a group comes from the philosopher John Dewey, the father of much of our educational thinking. Dewey advocated for democracy not as an abstract philosophical ideal, but as the key ingredient for personal growth, for innovation, and for progress.[3]

Frequently, a school system's central office makes a strategic plan and decides on the goals and the pace that schools need to follow to reach those goals. Even in these cases, there is still room for local decision making. Your school can still decide which parts of the system's plan you are going to tackle, how you are going to approach it, the training or support everyone needs, or which parts should come first and which parts should be saved for later. You usually don't have to do it all simultaneously or accomplish it all immediately. In fact, if you try to do everything, people will burn out. If you try to do it too fast, they will stress out. They have to feel that "you"—the plural you, the team "you"—have some control over your destiny.

When your staff sees that they are helping move the school ahead, you begin to pick up momentum, because it feels good as you start to succeed. Those positive feelings always translate into generating new ideas and increased efforts. It feels deeply satisfying to help make the decisions that resulted in those achievements because you have collectively been responsible for them.

It's also important to show everyone how far you've already come. Whether through data displayed on graphs, tables of survey results, or reports of focus groups and interviews, keeping track of your progress and making your results visible helps people look back objectively. Then everyone can reflect and make new decisions or modify their approaches if needed and appreciate the distance they have traveled. The education researcher Mike Schmoker reminds us that "all results—good or bad—are ultimately good, because they provide feedback that can guide us, telling us *what to do next* and how to do it better."[4] You are motivated to keep up your momentum when you see your progress.

Last but not least, you can remind everyone that it's their teamwork that has been the key. Betty Collins, the South Lake Elementary School principal we talked about in Chapter 2 as a model of optimism, used to sign every letter and column: "Together we make the difference." That was one of her ways of reminding everyone that they were making progress by joining hands and working together.

Going forward as a team says something about who you are and what you believe. In a school, it models for students that this is the way adults work together to accomplish great things. In any organization, it's what professionals do when they are at their best. Always **Move Together**; it's the only way to go.

On the other hand, I once knew a principal who thought she could move by herself. For example, she required all teachers to hang a poster on their front blackboard. It read: "Objectives: The student will know and be able to do . . ."

Her intention was excellent: to make sure that each teacher communicated the objectives of the lesson to the students. But let's look at how she did it. It was a classic top-down decision. She required it, so the clerical staff carefully printed the posters and laminated them. Every teacher dutifully hung the poster on the front blackboard and wrote some sort of objective following the three dots. Even beyond the fact that it wasn't very well thought out since you can't write a grammatically correct sentence with that stem, the real problem was that there was no sense of ownership of this initiative. The teachers hadn't agreed this was important to do. The Leadership Team hadn't decided it was crucial to the start of an effective lesson. Only the principal had decided. Was her decision based on solid research about the need to communicate objectives to children? Of course it was. But what was the result? And at what cost?

The teachers wrote something on their blackboards, reluctantly. Usually what they wrote wasn't much of an objective; sometimes it was just a topic—"Fractions," "The Korean War"—words that gave the students no more information about their learning than they had before. Sometimes they wrote something and left if up for a week or longer. If they were being formally observed by the principal, then they wrote a specific objective. But on the other days they often forgot to do it or wrote the absolute minimum.

What about students' achievement? It stayed about the same. And what happened to the principal? She left after three years, without much accomplished, without much contributed, without a positive legacy for the next principal to build on. The staff and parents said she cared mostly about appearances. While I believe that, in her heart, she cared about her students and their learning, she never got the school moving together. Unlike Duke Ellington, she certainly did not lead by participating, and that made it impossible to move together.

Teachers sometimes decide to collaborate without waiting for anyone else. The high-school social studies department decided to **Move Together** years before I arrived as the new principal. Guided by their department head, Freda Heisser, they worked out a plan to give students make-up tests before and after school and during lunch, with each teacher volunteering to take turns proctoring about once every two weeks. If a student needed a make-up test, the teacher simply put the student's name on the exam and put it in a folder in the department office. Students had three days to make up a test and there were no excuses. After all, they had nine opportunities within the three days.

The teachers also decided that if students were misbehaving, it was the department's responsibility to work it out. Take Joe, a sophomore student who is constantly talking and won't do his work. In most schools, typically, the teacher would talk with

Joe and then with his parents and, if the problem couldn't be resolved, Joe would get sent to the principal's office. But in this social studies department, the teacher would send Joe to talk with the head of the department, Freda. If he was still uncooperative, Freda would get Joe's schoolwork and assign him temporarily to another social studies teacher where he would be required to sit in a desk at the back of another class—a strategically chosen well-behaved class, a class which would ignore anyone trying to distract them. Usually it didn't take long before Joe would decide to be more cooperative.

The social studies teachers had made a firm decision to help each other move forward. Not only did they have an agreed-upon process in place for make-up exams and for students who misbehaved, they went much further. The teachers who taught the same courses thought of themselves as course-alike teams. They planned syllabi and lessons together, wrote tests together, created assignments together, and graded student work together —all ways to make sure that everyone was moving ahead together. As we read in Chapter 12's lesson on the Beatles, **Use Teamwork**, they were what Rick DuFour[5] and many others would now call a *professional learning community* before we knew the term for it. Were we surprised when the department's test scores rose dramatically as the years went by? Not at all.

An individual teacher can also send a message that the whole class is going to **Move Together**.

Currently, the instructional strategy named cooperative learning[6] is somewhat out of fashion, which is particularly surprising since cross-functional or ad-hoc teams are so prevalent in the business and non-profit sectors. A vice-president of Lockheed Martin once explained to me that the company credited their new strategy to review RFPs (requests for proposals) by using temporary ad-hoc teams, with members drawn from different departments, with avoiding multi-million-dollar mistakes in underbidding for government contracts.

Great teachers who create classrooms in which all students learn and in which everybody is committed to everyone's success almost always use some form of cooperative learning. Grading can be individualized so, in the end, students are graded on what they learn and accomplish individually. But that is a separate issue from helping one another to make sure that everyone is achieving. In an emotionally healthy and productive classroom, it is considered an honor to be a student who helps the teacher by tutoring others. Whether it's cross-age tutoring (older teaching younger students), peer tutoring (same age), or activities in which students become "experts" on a portion of the material and then help everyone learn the concepts, in the end the structure hardly matters. What does matter is that everyone believes that every person in the class is going to learn the material at a high level and that the teacher and students are not going to give up on anyone. Classes like that achieve. They learn and **MOVE TOGETHER.**

Notes

1   Examples of inclusive processes include: the Baldrige Process, see http://www.nist.gov/baldrige/about/index.cfm, and the Comer Process, see http://www.schooldevelopmentprogram.org/about/works.aspx.

2   Smith, M. K. 2001. Kurt Lewin, Groups, Experiential Learning and Action Research. *Encyclopedia of Informal Education*, http://www.infed.org/thinkers/et-lewin.htm.

3   Dewey, J. 1916. *Democracy and Education*. Macmillan. London.

4   Schmoker, M. 1999. *Results: The Key to Continuous School Improvement*. 2nd edition. ASCD. Alexandria, VA. P. 3.

5   Dufour, R. and Eaker, R. 1998. *Professional Learning Communities at Work: Best Practices for Enhancing Student Achievement*. Solution Tree Press. Bloomington, IN.

6   See http://www.co-operation.org/home/introduction-to-cooperative-learning/.

7   Lewin, K. 1936. *Principles of Topological Psychology*. McGraw-Hill. New York.

Reflection Activity 13

The whole is greater than the sum of its parts.

Kurt Lewin, psychologist[7]

The melding harmonies and seamless movements of the Temptations made them even greater as a group than as the talented individuals they were. Kurt Lewin, one of the pioneers of modern social and organizational psychology and who coined the term *group dynamics*, would certainly agree. He maintained that a group is more than the sum of its individual members.

In **Leadership Lesson 13: Move Together**, we saw this phenomenon play out in Freda Heisser's social studies department, where individual teachers collaborated in their planning and in their work with students to produce better results than they had ever accomplished as individuals.

We also learned that there are some key ways to help a team move together. First, even in a top-down organizational structure, there are opportunities to make collaborative decisions about how to implement the central office mandates. Your team can move together by prioritizing and pacing the changes you are required to make. Second, you can show everyone their progress by making your results visible. Third, you can remind everyone that the improvements are only occurring because of excellent teamwork. Inevitably, the progress produces positive feelings which translate into generating new ideas and increased efforts. By putting into place all of these steps, you not only **Move Together**, you start moving faster, picking up increased momentum with each new success.

Who do you know who has demonstrated **Leadership Lesson 13: Move Together**? What did they do and say? Be as specific as possible. What did you learn from them that you want to apply to your own life and work?

_____

_____

_____

_____

_____

_____

_____

_____

_____

_____

_____

_____

_____

_____

Reflect further by doing the self-rating scales below. If this leadership lesson is one you have just started using, you are at the beginning phase. If you are using this leadership lesson regularly, you are now at the practicing phase. Like expert musicians we need to commit to practicing these lessons for our entire careers and lives. When you have mastered this leadership lesson and incorporated it naturally into your repertoire, you have reached the leading level.

Rate yourself using this scale. Mark a place on the line that represents _your_ current state on **Leadership Lesson 13: Move Together**.

1	2	3	4	5
Beginning		Practicing		Leading

Rate your team, department, school, office, business, or organization using this scale. Mark a place on the line that represents *your group*'s current state on **Leadership Lesson 13: Move Together**.

1	2	3	4	5

Beginning   Practicing   Leading

What commitment will you and the people with whom you work make to your fulfillment of this leadership characteristic? How can you incorporate the leadership lesson **Move Together** into your life and work? What concrete action steps will you take? What will be the sequence? What timeline will you follow?

Commitment:

_____

_____

_____

_____

_____

_____

Action Steps	Person(s) Responsible	Timeline

Louis Armstrong

LESSON 14:
Be Yourself

Louis Armstrong
Credit: Library of Congress Prints and Photographs Division, New York World-Telegram and the Sun Newspaper Photograph Collection. 1953. Digital ID cph.3c27236. Retrieved from en.wikipedia.org/wiki/File: Louis_Armstrong_restored.jpg

LISTEN TO LOUIS ARMSTRONG play and sing. You are always struck by his naturalness, his lack of pretentiousness. He was undoubtedly a superb musician, yet there is no sense of ego or conceit—only joy in the music and the performance. Whether he's playing "When the Saints Go Marching In" New Orleans' style, singing and swinging "Mack the Knife," performing a duet with Bing Crosby in the movie *High Society*, or recording songs from Gershwin's *Porgy and Bess* with Ella Fitzgerald, he is always authentic, always himself. He is so at ease being who he is. As we listen, we all become so comfortable in his warm musical embrace of the whole wonderful world. This is the leadership lesson we learn from the unique and original Louis Armstrong, a lesson which encapsulates all the other lessons in this book and is paradoxically both the simplest and yet the most difficult to accomplish:

BE YOURSELF

The Lesson Goes to School: How Educators Can Be Themselves

Armstrong said it best: "You blows who you is." Journalist Sara Lukinson of the *Washington Post* called this "the most jampacked description of making art I've come across, including the art of living your life."[1]

The Swiss psychologist C. G. Jung wouldn't have been surprised that the objective of becoming truly oneself is the culminating lesson of *Lead Like the Legends*. Earlier in his career, Jung was a disciple of Sigmund Freud, but he came to believe that Freud's emphasis on sexual impulses and repressed feelings was too simple and too negative a way to view human nature.

Jung maintained, to become whole, a person needs to go through *individuation*,[2] a completely natural psychological process in which he or she integrates the conscious and unconscious personality. The goal of therapy, Jung said, is to help someone gain or regain his or her "own self." He observed that a person who makes progress in integrating his or her psyche in this way tends to be harmonious, mature, and responsible, embodying humane values such as freedom and justice and having a deep understanding of human nature.³ This is the type of person who has the characteristics we hope to find in our leaders.

Much has been written applying Jung's work on psychological types to management theory. Effective leaders need to have a deep understanding of their co-workers as well as of themselves. In **Leadership Lesson 12: Use Teamwork**, we saw how the Myers-Briggs, one of the most widely used personality inventories, can help a leader build a high-functioning team, as long as the leader has a deep enough understanding of human nature to value individuals' different strengths and knows how to include them to foster real teamwork. Only a leader with a fully integrated personality—an authentic self—can pull this off.

When I was in training to become a principal, we heard a message from one of our associate superintendents, a man with the unusual name of Dr. Hiawatha Fountain. By the time he talked to us, Dr. Fountain was in the last years of a long and storied career in school administration and had seen a lot of principals come and go, succeed and fail.

His advice to us up-and-comers was simple: "Don't stop being who you are. Just because you have a new position as a principal," he said,

don't forget all of the things you've always done that have helped you be successful. When you were a teacher, and you must have been good teachers to have been promoted to this position of leadership, you reached out to your students and their parents. You made yourself approachable. You made your classroom inviting. You listened to your students to try to figure out what they needed. If they didn't understand a lesson one way, you found another way to teach it. When you didn't know what to do, you asked other teachers for advice. You committed yourself because you really wanted your students to learn. You would do whatever it took for that to happen. You made sure it was all about them—not about you. When people get promoted to positions of leadership, they sometimes forget these lessons of their own past. They get a new office, a big desk, a secretary. Everyone defers to them because of their new authority. Don't let these surface things distract you. Be who you were before your promotion. Be who you've always been. That's what made you successful in your former jobs. That's what will make you successful in this job.

Dr. Fountain's advice is still sound. Remember who you are and don't change that fundamental, authentic person. For us, as future principals, it was a reminder that we had always been devoted to children. He said, "You always were the type of person who puts yourself second and the needs of the kids first. That's who the best school people are. That's who you are. And that's who you need to be as a leader."

Remembering who you are is also an essential element of **Leadership Lesson 9: Put the Message Across**, where we learned from Jim Collins[4] that the majority of the most effective leaders he studied turned out not to be famous hot-shot management wonder kids brought in from the outside, but humble, homegrown, loyal employees who worked their way up and sincerely wanted their company or organization to succeed. They were effective leaders whose co-workers trusted their decisions because they knew them—knew their personalities, their values, their whole selves.

It's also true that the school, department, or organization you lead becomes a reflection of your personality—an embodiment of your identity—your strengths, your weaknesses, your preferences, your avoidances, your interests, your values, your prejudices, your commitments, your wishes, your fulfillments, your regrets. You never completely control the environment, but, in a sense, you become part of one another. If you are a teacher, your classroom becomes you. If you are a principal, your school becomes you. Since there is no way to avoid that happening (and you shouldn't wish to avoid it anyway), it places the responsibility squarely on your shoulders. Be the person you want to be because you want your classroom, school, or team to become what it is capable of being. Everyone takes a page from the leader's book because the leader is the model. If you are at peace with yourself, if you are grounded in your values, then the people who work with you will not only have confidence in you, but they will have the self-confidence to be themselves and therefore will be their best selves.

We learned about the powerful idea called *self-efficacy* from the psychologist Albert Bandura[5] in **Leadership Lesson 3: Accept No Limits**. People of all ages can increase their belief in what they can accomplish. One of the most important ways to help others gain self-confidence is to give them the opportunity to learn from inspiring leaders who are authentically themselves.

Artie Shaw was a talented jazz clarinetist and band leader in his own right. His memory of his first encounter with the matchless Louis Armstrong demonstrates how he was influenced by Armstrong's example. He said,

I waited and I sat on a rug covered bandstand and waited and he came out. The first thing he played was *West End Blues*. And I heard this cascade of notes coming out of a trumpet. No one had ever done that before. And so I was obsessed with the idea that this is what you had to do, something that was your own, that had nothing to do with anybody else. I was influenced by him. Not in terms of notes, but in terms of the idea of doing what you are, who you are.[6]

Fourth-grade teacher Joseph Andrews was always authentically himself, and he affected hundreds of his students' lives and thousands more through the many teachers who were influenced by him. He changed our younger son's life.

Ben was a tall, skinny nine-year-old. He had always liked school, but there was a marked change in him when he started fourth grade in Mr. Andrews' class. He no longer *liked* school; he *loved* school. He would come home and tell my wife, Joanie, everything that happened in school that day. "Mr. Andrews' favorite animal is a moose." "Mr. Andrews read us a funny Shel Silverstein book. Can we get it from the library?" "Mr. Andrews taught us that the streams right near our town take water all the way to the Chesapeake Bay." When I came home in the evening, he would tell me all the same stories again, with just as much enthusiasm. The next morning he couldn't wait to get up and go to school to see what Mr. Andrews had planned for them.

In late September, South Lake Elementary announced its back-to-school night. Joanie and I were looking forward to going. We wanted to meet Mr. Andrews, to learn more about this man who had such a profound influence on our son.

I had been a teacher for many years and had given a lot of back-to-school night presentations to parents. Joanie and I had attended back-to-school nights for both of our sons, so we had heard a lot of these speeches. No matter how good the teachers were with kids, they were usually a little nervous speaking to parents, but mainly the speeches followed a typical pattern: a description of the curriculum, an overview of the class, a message that we were partners and communication was a two-way street, and a reminder that we should send in a box of tissues and a field-trip permission slip. I had already been a principal for a few years and had heard hundreds of back-to-school night presentations by my staff. I thought I had pretty much heard it all. But I was wrong. Mr. Andrews' back-to-school night talk was the best I had ever heard. While I can't replicate it here on the page as well as he gave it in person, I'll try my best to give you the essence of what he said.

All the parents made their way down the hall to Mr. Andrews' fourth-grade classroom. It looked like most classes in any elementary school, with the desks lined up behind each other in straight rows. After we had each sat down in one of the little chairs, Mr. Andrews stood up. He was short, with reddish-brown hair over his ears and forehead and a reddish-brown mustache and beard—he had the look of a grown-up child of the 1960s. If you passed him on the street, you probably wouldn't notice him. Yet this was the man who had made such an impression on our son.

"Good evening parents. Welcome to South Lake's Back-to-School Night," he said. "I want you to know that there is no place in the world that I would rather be than here at our school teaching your children."

In all the years I had given my own back-to-school night talks or heard other teachers give theirs, I had never heard such a heartfelt statement. I was very moved. He went on, "Now I'd like to tell you something about how I operate my classroom."

Because I had been an administrator for a while, I knew code language when I heard it. When teachers say they want to tell you about "how they operate their classrooms" that is actually code for: "I'm going to tell you the rules in my class." So although he had started out with such a touching opening remark, I could see that the speech was about to go downhill. Again, I was mistaken.

He continued, "This year your children are going to learn so much about reading, math, social studies, and science, but what I really want you to know is this. Do you see how you are each sitting in an individual desk and all the desks are in rows? Well, by the end of the first marking period, I will push the desks together so that the children are sitting in pairs. At the end of the second marking period, I will put the desks together in groups of four or six. By the third marking period, they will be in groups of eight or ten. And for the last marking period, all of the desks in the room will be moved together so that they will form one big table." He held his arms out with the palms of his hands parallel to the floor so we could picture the desks forming one long table. "It will be like a large dining room table and I'll be sitting at the head of the table like a father. You see, every year I try to create the feeling in my classroom that we are a family, living and learning together. And although I've only known your children for a few weeks, I can tell it's going to happen this year too."

We had never heard anything like this at a back-to-school night. No wonder our son loved being in this class with this teacher.

It was the year that Ben blossomed as a student. Every day he couldn't wait to go to school to share his thoughts with his teacher and to hear what the teacher had in store for them. That was the year of the Winter Olympics in Nagano, Japan. Mr. Andrews gave them an interesting homework assignment to do over winter break. They were to learn all they could about the world by watching and reading about the Olympics. Where were the athletes from? What do you know about their countries? What is the climate like in Japan? What did you learn about math from the scoring and judging of events? As he went back to school in January, Ben had an entire box of newspaper clippings and notes he had taken about the Olympics. He couldn't wait to show them to Mr. Andrews. He had learned so much about the world.

Fast forward eight years. Ben was ready to graduate high school. The tall, skinny nine-year-old was now 18 and six foot five. Because we live in the Washington, D.C. area, his high school held its graduation ceremony at D.A.R. Constitution Hall, just down the street from the White House; the same D.A.R. Constitution Hall that initially prevented Marian Anderson from singing on its stage, as we learned in **Lesson 7: Be Strong by Being Principled**, although when they finally changed their prejudiced policy, she gave a concert there.

It was a hot and sunny June day. Along with all the other hundreds of families we stood out on the sidewalk, waiting for the doors of the hall to open. As we waited, we helped our son put on his cap and gown. We took his picture and then took many more with all our family and friends gathered around him.

A small man made his way through the crowd of students and their families. He had reddish-brown hair over his ears and forehead and a reddish-brown mustache and beard. Wearing a friendly smile, he walked up to our son who towered above him and said, "Hello Ben."

Ben bent from the waist to get a closer look at this man from his past and, with an ear-to-ear grin and a combination of surprise and reverence in his voice, exclaimed, "Mr. Andrews!"

"Hi Ben. Hello Mr. and Mrs. Steinberg. You might have heard that I'm going to be moving to a different school next year and I'm planning to retire soon. Ben's will be the last graduating class I'll have taught, so I just wanted to come and see them one more time."

Then he did something that surprised us. Because he had the style of a man who had come of age in the 1960s, over his shoulder he was wearing a long leather pouch. He slowly reached into it and pulled out little 3x5 photographs of nine-year-old Ben and all his classmates from the time they had been lucky enough to have been in Mr. Joseph Andrews' fourth-grade class. You see, he meant it when he said that there was no place in the world that he would rather be than teaching our children.

People like Joseph Andrews who are authentically themselves have a powerful influence on others, and they are never forgotten. In high school, Ben became a camp counselor and discovered that he really enjoyed working with children. After college, he joined Teach for America and worked for two years in an alternative high school in Baltimore, designed for kids who had already dropped out of school once and were now back for a second chance. He found the work so meaningful that he continued teaching in a Baltimore charter high school. When we look back on his early formative experiences, we can't help but remember that he was lucky to have had great teachers like Joseph Andrews, who modeled the importance of **Being Yourself** and kindergarten teacher Brenda Robbins who taught him to **Accept No Limits** (as we learned in Chapter 3) and so many more that they could fill a book in themselves. When Ben had taught for a few years he began coaching the boys' basketball team, and we could see, in the way he sought to understand each player's needs, the influence of the coach he played for in high school—a man who helped him develop as a student, as an athlete, and as a young man.

In addition to modeling, another way people who are authentically themselves influence us is through their generosity. When you are completely comfortable with yourself, in your own way of being and living, you have a reservoir of energy to share with others.

When I was starting out as a teacher, I used to play piano in bars and restaurants and at private parties to supplement my meager teacher's salary and be able to pay our mortgage and bills and still have a little left over to occasionally take my wife to dinner and a movie. Every once in a while I had the chance to play with a really great musician. One day I was practicing in our Washington, D.C. apartment and our friend Kathy dropped by. She brought her dad, a retired Long Island firefighter who played saxophone in dance bands on the weekends. He brought his sax over and we played together for a while; just the two of us improvising our way through some old jazz standards, or, as he put it, "just noodling around."

We sounded pretty good, and when we played Duke Ellington's "Satin Doll" I noticed that I was playing much better than I ever had before. Why? I was never a serious musician and yet, with this old-time sax player, I could have been mistaken for a professional. I started listening more closely. Then I realized what was really happening.

It wasn't me. I was still the same amateur, "play a little on the weekends" piano player I was the ten minutes before the sax man walked in and opened his case. The difference was definitely him and what he was doing. He was making me sound better than I was. How was he doing it?

I noticed that when he would take a solo, and it was time for me to come in and take mine, when he realized that I wasn't sure about exactly when to start playing, he just held his note a little longer, so that whenever I started the piano solo it sounded like it was meant to be that way. And if I didn't know how to end the song, he heard some clue in my playing or watched my hands and body language, and made sure to end exactly when I did. To any listener it would have appeared as if we had musical telepathy and were perfectly synchronized. What he was doing was an act of generosity which not only made me seem somewhat skilled, but more importantly, we sounded better together than I ever thought possible.

Over the years, I noticed that all the best musicians do this— play with a generosity that brings out the best in everyone in the band. If there was ever a perfect metaphor for leadership, it's what happens in an experienced jazz combo. The musicians agree on the song and the tempo, but then there are improvisations and taking turns in leadership and being in the spotlight. You need to support each other. You have to feel your way through the song—to know if there is going to be another verse or a repeat of the chorus. You have to be sensitive to the way the song moves and to how each other adjust. As musicians aptly say, "You have to hear the changes." When you're successful, you make the changes together so seamlessly that the audience thinks it must have been planned that way all along. To do all this, you have to understand each other deeply and thoroughly because, as Louis Armstrong said, "You blows who you is." You support each other with the generosity of spirit that brings out the best in everyone. When you can **Be Yourself** while working with others, great things can be accomplished.

We began this book with our first legend, Judy Garland, who once offered some advice that applies perfectly to Louis Armstrong and his belief that "You blows who you is," as well as to every other musician in *Lead Like the Legends*.

Judy said, "Always be a first-rate version of yourself, instead of a second-rate version of someone else."[7]

BE YOURSELF. Being true to your authentic self is the best way to begin to incorporate every leadership lesson into your repertoire. Be the finest, first-rate version of yourself that you can be. Then you will be a leader who moves your classroom, your school, or your organization forward and makes a real difference in people's lives.

Notes

1 Lukinson, S. 2005. A Serving of Jealousy. *Washington Post*. September 5, www.washingtonpost.com/wp-dyn/content/article/2005/09/04/AR2005090401311.html.

2 Jung's Individuation Process. Retrieved March 2, 2014 from http://soultherapynow.com/articles/individuation.html.

3 Jung, C. G. and Campbell, J. 1976. *The Portable Jung*. Translated by R. F. C. Hull. Penguin Books. New York.

4 Collins, Jim. 2001. *Good to Great*. HarperCollins. New York.

5 Bandura, Albert. 1986. *Social Foundations of Thought and Action: A Social Cognitive Theory*. Prentice-Hall. Englewood Cliffs, NJ.

6 Burns, K. 2001. *Jazz*. PBS. Boston, MA.

7 Kennedy, Lou. 1992. *Business Etiquette for the Nineties: Your Ticket to Career Success*. Palmetto. Charleston, SC. P. 8.

8 Shakespeare, William. *Hamlet*, Act 1, Scene 3. P. 3, http://shakespeare.mit.edu/hamlet/hamlet.1.3.html.

9 Burns, *Jazz*.

Reflection Activity 14

This above all: to thine own self be true,
And it must follow, as the night the day,
Thou canst not then be false to any man.
                    Hamlet,[8] by William Shakespeare

In his ground-breaking documentary *Jazz*,[9] Ken Burns profiles Louis Armstrong through his long career as one of the transformative figures of American music. Throughout all his years of music-making fame, Armstrong followed Shakespeare's advice; he stayed true to himself. No matter the setting, he played and sang with his unmistakable sound, immediately recognizable to this day. He also remained married to the same woman and together they continued to live in their modest home in Queens, New York.

The psychologist C. G. Jung said that the purpose of life is to integrate our psyches and become our "own selves" so that we can become mature and generous and embrace humane values such as freedom and justice. When Louis Armstrong was older and thought of by many younger musicians as an uncool retro voice of the past, he kept true to his music and his values. In 1957, he was the only jazz musician to speak out in protest when the governor of Arkansas failed to protect the first nine black students integrating Central High School.

Teachers like Joseph Andrews who are authentically themselves influence their students' lives and are always remembered for their knowledge, insightfulness, care, and generosity. Like the best musicians playing in a jazz combo, when you, as a leader, can **Be Yourself** while working harmoniously with others, you bring out the best in everyone as individuals and in the group as a whole.

In your life and work, who has demonstrated **Leadership Lesson 14: Be Yourself**? What did they do and say? Be as specific as possible. What did you learn from them that you want to apply to your own life and work?

_____

_____

_____

_____

_____

_____

_____

_____

_____

_____

_____

_____

_____

_____

_____

_____

Reflect further by doing the self-rating scales below. If this leadership lesson is one you have just started using, you are at the beginning phase. If you are using this leadership lesson regularly, you are now at the practicing phase. Like expert musicians we need to commit to practicing these lessons for our entire careers and lives. When you have mastered this leadership lesson and incorporated it naturally into your repertoire, you have reached the leading level.

Rate yourself using this scale. Mark a place on the line that represents _your_ current state on **Leadership Lesson 14: Be Yourself**.

1	2	3	4	5
Beginning		Practicing		Leading

Rate your team, office, school, business, or organization using this scale. Mark a place on the line that represents *your group*'s current state on **Leadership Lesson 14: Be Yourself**.

1	2	3	4	5

Beginning	Practicing	Leading

What commitment will you and the people with whom you work make to fulfill this leadership characteristic? How can you incorporate the leadership lesson of **Being Yourself** into your life and work? What concrete action steps will you take? What will be the sequence? What timeline will you follow?

Commitment:

_____

_____

_____

_____

_____

_____

Action Steps	Person(s) Responsible	Timeline

Coda

Although this began as a book about leadership for teachers and other educators, it soon became apparent that the lessons can be universally applied. From parents teaching their children to managers mentoring the next generation of employees, our ideas of leadership define us.

We have now learned about leadership from 14 great musical legends. I chose them because I have a personal affection for them and their music and because they have something important to teach us. I'm convinced that you could choose inspiring legends from any field that resonates with you—history, sports, art, science—and find lessons of leadership in their lives and work.

By now, I'm sure it is as clear to you as it is to me that the real legends described in this book are not only the famous musicians. They are the people who have lived the leadership lessons in their own lives—the teachers, principals, and other staff who exercised leadership on behalf of the children in their care. They are heroes, not enjoying the spotlight of celebrity, but committed to making people's lives better.

The lessons the leaders use to help people improve their lives—their professional lives and their personal lives—aren't linear. Although the lessons in *Lead Like the Legends* are numbered 1–14, there isn't a recommended first-you-do-this and then-you-do-that sequence. The lessons overlap and reinforce each other. A leader using a strategy primarily rooted in one of the lessons is often simultaneously using ideas stemming from several of the other lessons as well.

For example, it is important that leaders unify the groups of people for whom they are responsible (**Leadership Lesson 11: Unify**). This is just one thread that weaves through all of the leadership lessons in *Lead Like the Legends*.

Principal Sharon Jones kept the families of her school **unified** throughout the disruption caused by the destruction of a low-rent apartment complex. Her **sincerity** convinced parents that she and her staff would support them and provide them with stability through a time of uncertainty in which they didn't know where they would live or where their children would go to school (**Leadership Lesson 1: Be Sincere**).

Teacher Ann Pokoyk's **optimism** about her students' potential produced a **unified** and motivated class of sixth graders, even though many of them started out far below grade level in their skills (**Leadership Lesson 2: Be Optimistic**).

Three thousand people spontaneously rose from their seats to give a **unified** standing ovation to a boy with multiple physical disabilities as his motorized wheelchair sped across the graduation stage, because coordinator Denise Wilson **refused to accept the limits** of an inaccessible Constitution Hall from giving him a full graduation experience (**Leadership Lesson 3: Accept No Limits**).

Alternative education teacher Allie "Mama" Ground dug deep within herself to **find another way** to reach out to the brother of a dying student, earning the trust and **unifying** a group of at-risk students (**Leadership Lesson 4: Be Eclectic**).

Math department chair Becky Sanderoff **led by example** and **unified** the teachers in her department by teaching the students with the weakest skills and suffering the same inconveniences as the newest teachers (**Leadership Lesson 5: Lead by Participating**).

Principal John Cessini **imagined** that the arts could **unify** an elementary school and put it on the map (**Leadership Lesson 6: Lead with Imagination**).

Coach Paul Foringer's **strongly held values** helped him **unify** his varsity basketball team around the characteristics of being both good students and good athletes, and lead his team to a state championship (**Leadership Lesson 7: Be Strong by Being Principled**).

Peggy Bastien **unified** her fourth graders as a class that learned at ever higher levels by **building her own capacity** as a teacher (**Leadership Lesson 8: Train to Grow**).

Counselor Alison Senghor's **selfless** approach to leadership **unified** the staff's focus on designing a mentoring program for young boys (**Leadership Lesson 9: Put the Message Across**).

Middle-school principal Eric Davis **unified** his staff by energetically leading a transformation of his school's climate by **daring** to promise peace days (**Leadership Lesson 10: Be Daring and High Energy**).

High-school principal Carole Working made it personal and used her belief that every student should graduate and have access to life's opportunities as a way to **unify** a large staff around that mission (**Leadership Lesson 11: Unify**).

Sixth-grade team leaders Anita Prince and Margy Hall **unified** their middle-school teaching **teams** by building trust and drawing on **each** person's contribution (**Leadership Lesson 12: Use Teamwork**).

The most successful teachers **unify** their classrooms when they communicate that **every student** is going to learn at the highest levels and then encourage their students to help teach each other (**Leadership Lesson 13: Move Together**).

Fourth-grade teacher Joseph Andrews was always **authentically himself**, which helped him to **unify** his students so completely that every year his classroom felt like a family learning and living together (**Leadership Lesson 14: Be Yourself**).

As we see in these examples, the **unity** that people long for became a by-product of a leader simultaneously employing strategies based on the other lessons. The same is true for **Train to Grow, Use Teamwork, Move Together**, or any of the other leadership lessons. A focus on one becomes a catalyst for progress in the others.

When the poet Ralph Waldo Emerson described a successful life[1] he might have also been capturing the essence of the characteristics of a successful leader we have learned together in *Lead Like the Legends*.

To laugh often and much; to win the respect of intelligent people and the affection of children; to earn the appreciation of honest critics and endure the betrayal of false friends; to appreciate beauty; to find the best in others; to leave the world a bit better, whether by a healthy child, a garden patch or a redeemed social condition; to know even one life has breathed easier because you lived. This is to have succeeded.

Now it's your turn. There are people counting on you to be the leaders they need. Act with **sincerity** and **optimism** about their futures and **accept no limits** on their potential or your own; use an **eclectic** range of strategies and **lead by participating** alongside them; use **your imagination** to be creative and **stay strong by holding fast to your principles**; continuously **train to grow** professionally and personally and **put the message across** instead of yourself; act with **daring and high energy** and **unify** people and their ideas; inspire **teamwork** with a group that **moves together**, and most importantly, always **be authentically yourself**.

You can and will be a legend, a leader they will always remember with respect, gratitude, and love.

Share Your Legends

We all have legends that have made a difference in our lives. Share the stories of the people that have inspired you. Send their stories to me on Facebook or at steinbergdavidi@gmail.com so that others can be inspired too.

Testimonials

Contact David Steinberg

You can contact David Steinberg for keynotes, professional development, workshops, or consulting on Facebook, LinkedIn, or at steinbergdavidi@gmail.com.

Participants' Comments about
"Lead Like the Legends" Presentations

"Lead Like the Legends" by David Steinberg was entertaining, engaging, and inspiring! By the end of the workshop I had reflected through music the qualities of educational leadership that I need to grow over the remainder of my career. After the workshop concluded, I was motivated to do more as a leader of my school.

Andrew Winter, Principal,
Greencastle Elementary School

David's workshop will keep your staff engaged from beginning to end. He weaves leadership qualities with music and anecdotes into a session that will inspire your teachers to be the very best they can be! One of my fourth grade teachers returned to the class the next day and used some of the very same strategies with her students. David's workshop was inspirational! If you want your staff to feel valued and have a wonderful time in doing so, this is the session for you!

Linda Goldberg, Principal,
Potomac Elementary School

Dr. Steinberg uses legends from the past to highlight important leadership characteristics that are essential to the effectiveness of today's school-based administrators.

Moreno Carrasco, Director,
Secondary Leadership Development

David Steinberg's "Lead Like the Legends" is an entertaining and insightful lesson in how popular standards in music can highlight exemplary cases of educational leadership. Dr. Steinberg's repartee is thoughtfully presented and his chosen leaders will provide true inspiration to all who attend his presentations.

Keith R. Jones, Principal,
Summit Hall Elementary School

We recently had the pleasure of inviting Dr. David I. Steinberg to a Potomac Elementary Staff meeting. Dr. Steinberg has been a teacher and principal. Dr. Steinberg presented a revue of songs by different composers, performers, and musicians. After each song was presented, the staff was treated to a short explanation of the origin of the song, a little biographical information about the famous musician or performer, and a leadership lesson showcased by the song or artist. Dr. Steinberg then related that leadership characteristic to a personal experience he had experienced in his career.

We talked about the power of being sincere and being optimistic, as fashioned in the songs, "Somewhere Over the Rainbow" and "Oh, What A Beautiful Morning." Upon hearing Ray Charles' rendition of "Georgia, On My Mind" we talked about the perseverance Ray Charles demonstrated in his life, and we made a connection to educators who should accept no limits, by teaching to each student's strength. We listened to "A Little Help from My Friends" by the Beatles, and discussed the great value in teamwork and collaboration. The song, "What a Wonderful World," performed by Louis Armstrong, highlighted how important it is for educators to be authentic and be themselves.

Our staff thoroughly enjoyed the presentation and the opportunity to think about the leadership qualities we possess and want to expand.

Ellen Winston, Staff Development Teacher,
Potomac Elementary School

"Lead Like the Legends" was a creative, entertaining, and fun session that certainly held the interest of our conference attendees. Feedback from participants indicated that it was the session "most frequently requested to be repeated" at the conference. David's ability to combine an enjoyable experience with learning was certainly demonstrated in this presentation.

Rebecca Newman, President, Montgomery County Association
of Administrative and Supervisory Personnel

David Steinberg's "Lead Like the Legends" is one of the most entertaining school leadership workshops in which I have ever participated. It is humorous and lively, yet teaches some great lessons about the work of school administrators. Some people might ask what David's going to do for an encore, but this performance needs no encore!

Don Kress, Chief School Performance Officer,
Montgomery County Public Schools

A refreshing, interactive, and thought-provoking session that offers the audience an entertaining opportunity to forge connections between the talents of legendary musical artists of our time and the gifts of the multi-faceted educational leaders.

Martin J. Barnett, Principal,
Cold Spring Elementary School

Every school improvement effort wants to define what excellent leadership looks like in our public schools. The researchers involved in these efforts want to know what it is in order to replicate those leaders. Dr. Steinberg's presentation brings the most agreed upon characteristics of that elusive leader to life. While *leadership* has proven difficult to define, when you see it, you know it. Dr. Steinberg leads you in the right direction so you can see it—and hear it! His inspiring presentation makes every educator want to be the very best leader in their school.

Hilarie Rooney, Principal,
Laytonsville Elementary School

David Steinberg's "Lead Like the Legends" workshop is highly interactive, fun and entertaining! Be ready to sing along! The presentation is a wonderful way to salute and inspire administrators and teachers alike!

Elaine L. Chang, Principal,
Lakewood Elementary School

By far, this was one of the best ways I've spent an afternoon. The music made the presentation fun, almost like we were playing a game. The stories shared were inspirational and boosted my spirits. I left the presentation feeling motivated and energized about my career and life in general. Thank you for bringing some "sunshine" to our school.

Carrie Walker, Teacher,
Lakewood Elementary School

Your presentation at our staff meeting was amazing!

Angie Henderson, Media Specialist,
Gaithersburg Elementary School

I was tongue-tied after your presentation because you are an impossible act to follow. Your "leadership lessons" will do more than help me "lead like the legends." They are qualities and characteristics that I want to have in all the roles that are part of my life.

This was an outstanding workshop that I hope we can present to all future members of Project CHANGE.

Thank YOU! Thank YOU!

Judy Lapping, Director,
Project CHANGE (AmeriCorps)

Today's presentation by Dr. Steinberg was excellent! The "Dr. Steinberg Leadership Experience" was as thoughtful as it was amusing. Music certainly adds to the appeal but, for me, the rich examples from life as a teacher and administrator are particularly memorable. Although the music of legendary musicians had a hand in him becoming a creative and inspired person, it would seem that he finds heroes in the people around him. I left today's presentation interested in finding some heroes of my own.

Lisa Maltz, AmeriCorps Member

Wow! The presentation was just fabulous! Several staff members commented on how much they enjoyed it. You definitely modeled "lead with imagination" and "train to grow." Various staff members possess at least one of the leadership qualities you shared, but I think your presentation had everyone personally reflecting on how *many* of the qualities we possess *and* demonstrate. It will be interesting to see how many more leadership qualities we begin to see additional people demonstrating around the school.

Thank you so much for taking time from your busy schedule to share your talents and insights!!

Patricia Calvin, NBCT, Staff Development Teacher,
GT Liaison, Woodfield ES

Thank you so much for your wonderful inspiring presentation yesterday. It is fantastic. Your words touched the inner teacher in everyone. As soon as I got home last night I had the email below in my mailbox from one of my students. Your time and efforts are making a difference for future teachers and most importantly future students.

Ellie Giles, Ed.D., Internship Coordinator,
Johns Hopkins University

Dr. Steinberg was an amazing speaker and the lecture was very motivating. Dr. Steinberg was so inspirational and his words were so moving to become the best teacher I can be. Thank you so much for encouraging people to come to the event. It was one of the best lectures I have ever been to.

Kristen Millios, Graduate Student,
Johns Hopkins University

Thank you very much for the high energy, creative and thought provoking presentation you gave Monday at South Lake ES. In so many wonderful ways, it was like a walk down memory lane for me as I sat listening to your flashbacks in time and "leadership lessons." Currently, I am a special education paraeducator with the Infants and Toddlers Program. "Everyone Is a Leader" taught me so much and I look forward to sharing the information I learned with my co-workers.

Nancy McCann, Special Education Paraeducator

To Whom It May Concern:

This letter is in reference to the services offered by Dr. David Steinberg, a longtime educator and colleague in the area of motivational speaking. Having known David for a number of years (we were High School Principals for a while together), I knew of his many talents, but had never seen him "in action" until this past fall at a statewide gathering of Maryland school board members. David was extraordinary in such a unique approach that I offered to write this recommendation. He is funny, adapts music to his message (David is an accomplished musician, playing numerous instruments), and due to his long career, has credibility with a variety of audiences. Teachers, administrators, and those involved with education can sometimes be a very difficult audience.

At the conclusion of his presentation, he received a standing ovation. I might add that he was the concluding presenter of a three-day conference, ending on a fall Friday in good weather (and no one left early)!

Should your Faculty, PTA, school system, or group be looking for a unique presentation, coupled with a very powerful message, David Steinberg is well worth looking into.

Michael A. Durso, Board of Education Member,
Montgomery County Board of Education

Thank you for a wonderfully inspirational and engaging presentation this morning. While so many staff development presentations strictly impart information, yours tugged at the heart strings and helped me to make meaningful connections with important leadership principles.

Douglas C. Elmendorf, Assistant Principal,
Dundalk Elementary School

I was one of the attendees this past week-end for the Maryland Business Education Association Conference held in Ocean City. Your keynote was outstanding and right on target for teachers. It was motivating and uplifting. Thank you for entertaining, but also teaching us how we can lead like the legends!

Leila G. Walker, Coordinator, Career and
Technology Education, Baltimore County Public Schools

Thank you for the outstanding presentation you provided for our new teachers. I am sure you enjoyed the enthusiastic reaction of the crowd, and your presentation provided the perfect closing message for our event. I appreciate your willingness to work us into your very busy schedule, and your stories and messages set just the right tone for getting new teachers ready for the challenging year ahead. Thanks again for helping us close our event with a message that was both entertaining and thought-provoking.

Deborah M. Piper, Coordinator, Teacher Development,
Department of Professional Development,
Baltimore County Public Schools

I attended the "Lead Like the Legends" session yesterday. I just wanted to thank you and tell you how much I enjoyed it. I not only had a great time but I walked away with a list of leadership skills I will be applying in my own classroom. Thank you. It was a great start to the day.

Rachel Pachtman, Family and Consumer Sciences Teacher,
Baltimore County Public Schools

Greetings . . . I attended Montgomery College's early childhood education event today and thoroughly enjoyed your presentation. I think this was the first time—certainly in my recent memory—that I enjoyed listening to a beginning of event keynote speaker. I'm kicking myself that I stopped playing the clarinet and piano. I could have used both with my students. Again, I enjoyed your presentation very much. We were rockin' at the end.

Karen Trebilcock, Adjunct Professor in ESL,
Montgomery College, Rockville, Maryland

"Dr. Steinberg's presentation was simply Awesome!!" "Wow! Dr. Steinberg was an absolutely amazing speaker—motivating and spoke such truths." "Today's session renewed my energy in every way." "I could go on and on . . . the list of accolades is very long."

Teachers, administrators, and parents participating
in a Professional Learning Communities Institute

You truly know how to connect with the staff and your message is so meaningful and relevant. Thank you for taking time from your busy schedule to speak to my staff. You are so talented and you're such a dynamic presenter. I can't wait to schedule you for "Lead Like the Legends, Part II." Below are some of the comments from our teachers as they reflected on the leadership lessons they learned in "Lead Like the Legends":

"What a fun way to be reminded about the importance of the work we do."

"Several of the leadership lessons stuck with me."

"I drove home thinking about teamwork and my team."

"I need to tell my students every day that they are the best so that they can believe it and act like it!"

"I loved the diverse examples he used musically and how the music connected to an idea. I can recall his leadership lessons because of the music legends he tied them to."

"Be present and passionate about what you do."

"We impact kids in more ways than we realize."

"Believe."

"Set your expectations high and don't lower them."

"When I got home I called my mom to tell her about the presentation and it just reminded me how important our job is and how cool it is to be able to make a difference in so many lives."

"I can't begin to think of all the incredible motivating speakers I have witnessed live in person from Joel Ostein at the Baltimore Civic Center, to Tony Robbins in Vegas, to David Steinberg today. Dr. Steinberg's show really hit home as to why I love what I do! I caught myself tearing up on a few occasions due to the stories that really hit home. I know I will utilize what I got from today by recognizing the leadership attributes as I deliver my lessons in class."

"I was at dinner with some friends this evening and I was so excited to share with them all about the many things he talked about. What a terrific way to begin the week and it reminded me of the importance of an educator in a child's life."

"Dr. Steinberg kept my, and the entire staff's, full attention with his musical activity and heart-felt stories."

"His examples were ones that I myself have in my head of great teachers and ones I hope in years to come, my students and parents would say about me. It really reinforces why we got into this profession."

"Overall . . . A+ presentation—I would recommend it to anyone."

"It helped me to be reflective and made me take a step back and think."

"The meeting energy left me in awe of how Dr. Steinberg made connections with music, thinking, cooperative conversations, famous role models, and teachers. He truly values education at every level and continues to give at his greatest capacity."

"So many of the lessons are demonstrated every day at this school. The people I work with here are sincere, optimistic, high energy, accept no limits, use teamwork and inspire me to follow their lead."

"I walked away thinking: What am I doing in my own life that leaves a breath of fresh air to others and leaves them feeling hopeful and more happy?"

Greg Edmundson, Principal,
Great Seneca Creek Elementary School

Thank you for coming to Great Seneca Creek. Your presentation on "Lead Like the Legends" is one that I will remember. I walked away with a deeper awareness of the importance and power of my job as an educator. Your examples of extraordinary leaders helped me to realize that what I do and say every day has a great impact on my students.

In addition, your story about Mr. Andrews really drove home the point that to lead like a legend, one has to genuinely care. By caring, one will naturally lead by participating and move everyone together as a team with sincerity and optimism. Just as Mr. Andrews has a deep impact on your son and family, when teachers lead well, we will naturally cultivate great leaders for the future.

Thank you again for an unforgettable presentation!
Uyen Vu Phillips, First-Grade Teacher,
Great Seneca Creek ES

I thoroughly enjoyed your presentation and learned a great deal about myself. The photos and your personal examples were quite an impressionable way to remember the traits of a great teacher.
Mary Ellen Kenealy, Physical Education Teacher,
Gaithersburg Middle School

You presented important information in a motivating and inspiring way. It truly lifted me up and helped me focus on the important work for the year.
Catherine Wright, English Teacher,
Gaithersburg Middle School

Thanks again for a wonderful morning session! I truly enjoy listening to you and am inspired by your thoughts and words.
Jennifer Pinsky-Newman, Teacher,
Baltimore County Public Schools

I just wanted to say thank you for coming to Neelsville today and giving your talk, "Lead Like the Legends." I have never heard anyone speak in such an engaging, emotional and poignant way to teachers. I really think you touched everyone in the room.

You were phenomenal, and have certainly given me inspiration to last for quite a while.

Kathleen Jacobs, Teacher, Neelsville Middle School

What a great surprise to see that you were the keynote speaker at Montgomery College today! I was there with two co-workers of mine and we couldn't stop raving about you! We thought you were an INCREDIBLE, engaging, talented, humorous and an uplifting speaker. I looked around the room at different times during the presentation and every single person was engaged, participating, and paying close attention.

Lori Hurwitz, Preschool Teacher